WeightWatchers®
BOOK OF RECIPES
MORE THAN 150 RECIPES

First published in Great Britain by Simon & Schuster UK Ltd, 2007
A CBS Company

First published 2007

Simon & Schuster UK Ltd, Africa House, 64-78 Kingsway, London WC2B 6AH

Weight Watchers Publications Team: Corrina Griffin, Jane Griffiths, Nina McKerlie and Nina Bhogal

Photography by Steve Baxter, Iain Bagwell and Steve Lee
Design and typesetting by Fiona Andreanelli
Printed and bound in China

A CIP catalogue for this book is available from the British Library

ISBN 0 7432 95501

Pictured on the front cover: Pear Brûlées page 113.
Pictured on the back cover: Fiery chicken pitta pockets page 24 (top left), Light spaghetti carbonara page 14 (top right), Chocolate chip cookies page 147 (bottom left), Thai fish curry page 122 (bottom right).

 You'll find this easy to read *POINTS*® value logo on every recipe throughout the book. The logo represents the number of *POINTS* values per serving each recipe contains. The easy to use *POINTS* plan is designed to help you eat what you want – as long as you stay within your daily *POINTS* allowance – giving you the freedom to enjoy the food you love.

V This symbol denotes a vegetarian recipe and assumes that, where relevant, organic eggs, vegetarian cheese and vegetarian low fat crème fraîche is used. Virtually fat free fromage frais may contain traces of gelatine so they are not always vegetarian. Please check the labels.

✳ This symbol denotes a dish that can be frozen.

Recipe notes:
All fruits, vegetables and eggs are medium sized unless otherwise stated.

Raw eggs: Only the freshest eggs should be used. Pregnant women, the elderly and children should avoid recipes with eggs that are not fully cooked or raw.

Recipe timings are approximate and meant to be guidelines. Please note that the preparation time includes all the steps up to and following the main cooking time (s).

Contents

Here, in one **fabulous** volume, is a special selection of favourite recipes from the hugely **successful** Weight Watchers programmes.

The recipes are **simple** and **easy** to follow, whether you're a novice cook or an expert – there's something for everyone and **inspiration** for all. There is no compromising on flavour and the quality of ingredients. Fresh herbs and produce are used throughout the recipes to give you healthy choices that taste great.

Everyone wants to **lose weight** in a way that suits their particular lifestyle. Weight Watchers helps you to do this with some simply delicious dishes and sensible indulgences that you can rustle up for yourself in no time, enjoy with family and friends or adapt from a favourite recipe, without compromising your weight-loss **goals**.

Little chocolate pots, page 34

Tuna melt

Takes 10 minutes

serves **2**   *POINTS* values per recipe **8.5**   calories per serving **335**

A substantial lunch for two, these tuna melts go down a treat with the kids, but you may wish to omit the capers.

4 medium slices of bread
150 g can of tuna in brine, drained
1 tablespoon Worcestershire sauce
125 g tub of low fat soft cheese
2 tablespoons capers
salt and freshly ground black pepper

❶ Preheat the grill and toast the bread on one side. Meanwhile, mix together all the other ingredients in a bowl.

❷ Divide the mixture into four and spread over the untoasted side of each slice of bread. Return to the grill for a couple of minutes until the topping turns golden brown.

VARIATION 1 Substitute Quark for the low fat soft cheese; the *POINTS* values per serving will be 3½.

VARIATION 2 Instead of capers, or in addition to the capers, you can add two sun dried tomatoes, soaked in boiling water for 5 minutes and then finely chopped. The *POINTS* values per serving will be 4½.

Spice rice with smoked haddock

Takes 25 minutes

serves **4**   *POINTS* values per recipe **17.5**   calories per serving **335**

This makes a starter for six or a breakfast for four.

200 g (7 oz) long grain rice
2 tablespoons medium curry powder
2 eggs
400 g (14 oz) smoked haddock fillets
300 ml (½ pint) fish or vegetable stock
low fat cooking spray
garlic
1 white onion, chopped
2 tablespoons chopped fresh parsley
2 tomatoes, each cut into 6 wedges
salt and freshly ground black pepper

❶ Put the rice and curry powder in a pan and cover with water. Bring to the boil, cover and simmer for 10 minutes.

❷ Meanwhile, hard boil the eggs for 8 minutes.

❸ Place the haddock and stock in a large frying pan, cover and cook for 6 minutes (until the fish flakes easily).

❹ Using the low fat cooking spray, cook the onion until just starting to brown.

❺ When the fish is cooked, skin and flake the flesh.

❻ When the eggs are cooked, plunge into cold water to cool and then remove the shells. Cut into wedges.

❼ When the rice is cooked, drain if necessary and then stir in a tablespoon of chopped parsley, the cooked onion and cooked fish. Season to taste.

❽ Garnish with wedges of egg and tomato. Sprinkle with the remaining parsley. Serve immediately.

(4½ POINTS VALUE) Eggs Benedict

Takes 20 minutes

serves **2** **POINTS** values per recipe **9** calories per serving **275**

A lower calorie version of an all time favourite breakfast dish; try making this for a weekend brunch treat.

1 teaspoon malt vinegar
2 eggs
1 English muffin, halved
2 teaspoons low fat spread
25 g (1 oz) wafer thin ham
1 tomato, sliced
2 tablespoons half fat crème fraîche
2 tablespoons Weight Watchers from Heinz 90% fat free mayonnaise
a pinch of paprika

❶ Pour enough water into a frying pan to come half way up the side of the pan. Add the vinegar and bring to the boil. Carefully crack the eggs (one at a time) into a cup and then slide the egg out carefully into the water. Poach for about 3 to 4 minutes, depending on how well you like your eggs cooked. Preheat the grill.

❷ Carefully lift the eggs out of the pan using a slotted spoon and drain on absorbent kitchen paper for 1 minute.

❸ Meanwhile, toast the muffin under the grill for 1 to 2 minutes per side, until golden. Spread with a little low fat spread and top with wafer thin ham and tomato slices.

❹ Lift an egg on top of each muffin half and then transfer to serving plates. Mix together the crème fraîche and mayonnaise and heat gently to just warm through but not bubble. Spoon over the eggs, sprinkle with paprika and serve at once.

(2½ POINTS VALUE) Mushroom sloppy joes

Takes 25 minutes

serves **4** **POINTS** values per recipe **10.5** calories per serving **130**   **V**

Sloppy Joes are a popular American dish, which are normally made with mince. This mushroom version is simply delicious!

350 g (12 oz) large button mushrooms, quartered
2 garlic cloves, crushed
low fat cooking spray
150 ml (5 fl oz) vegetable stock
290 g can of 99% fat free condensed mushroom soup
2 tablespoons half fat crème fraîche
4 medium slices of wholemeal bread
salt and freshly ground black pepper
1 tablespoon chopped fresh parsley, to garnish

❶ Place the mushrooms and garlic in a pan, spray with low fat cooking spray and cook them gently for 5 minutes.

❷ Add the stock and seasoning, and cook over a high heat for 5 minutes. Stir in the soup and heat through.

❸ Add the crème fraîche and stir well. Remove from the heat. Toast the bread.

❹ Top the four slices of toast with the mixture. Scatter over the parsley and serve.

VARIATION There is such a wide variety of mushrooms available in supermarkets. Try experimenting with different types such as oyster, shiitake or brown cap mushrooms.

(2) Oaty fruit biscuits

Takes 40 minutes

makes 6   *POINTS* values per recipe **13**   calories per serving **150**   V

120 g (4¼ oz) dried pears, chopped
grated rind of 1 lemon
6 tablespoons orange juice
150 g (5½ oz) rolled oats
low fat cooking spray

❶ Preheat the oven to Gas Mark 6/200°C/fan oven 180°C.

❷ Place the pears in a small pan with the lemon rind and orange juice. Bring to a gentle simmer and simmer for 8–10 minutes until the pears are softened and have absorbed half of the juice. Purée the pears and juice in a blender.

❸ Mix the purée with the oats. Spray a 20 cm (8 inch) loose bottomed tin with low fat cooking spray and press the mixture into the bottom of the tin. Bake for 18–20 minutes.

❹ Remove from the oven and cut into six wedges. Leave to cool in the tin.

VARIATION Most dried fruits work in this recipe: try apricots or prunes which make it a bit stickier. The *POINTS* values will be 1½ and 2 respectively.

(4½) French toast with mustard

Takes 10 minutes

serves 1   *POINTS* values per recipe **4.5**   calories per serving **325**   V

Try to use bread that's about two days old. Very fresh bread won't soak up the liquid very well.

2 medium slices of wholemeal bread
1 egg
½ teaspoon coarse grain mustard
150 ml (¼ pint) skimmed milk
½ teaspoon butter
salt and freshly ground black pepper

❶ Cut the bread slices in half diagonally.

❷ Beat together the egg, mustard and milk and season to taste. Pour into a shallow dish. Dip the bread slices in and leave to soak up the liquid.

❸ Heat the butter in a non stick frying pan and cook the soaked bread slices for 2 to 3 minutes per side, until golden. Serve at once.

(4) Cheesy hammy muffins

Takes 20 minutes

serves **2**   *POINTS* values per recipe **8.5**   calories per serving **260**

This is a delicious brunch dish for those special mid mornings when you have a little time on your hands.

150 g (5½ oz) baby spinach leaves
1 English muffin, split in half
30 g (1¼ oz) wafer thin ham
2 reduced fat cheese slices
1 teaspoon malt vinegar
2 large eggs
salt and freshly ground black pepper

❶ Place the spinach in a small saucepan with 2 tablespoons of water and a little seasoning. Cover and heat gently for 2 minutes until the spinach wilts.

❷ Meanwhile lightly toast the muffin halves and top each with wafer thin ham and a slice of cheese – keep them warm while poaching the eggs.

❸ Bring a large saucepan of water to the boil and add the vinegar. With the handle of a wooden spoon, swirl the water and, as you do so, crack in an egg – the swirling of the water helps the egg white stay together. Gently simmer for 2–3 minutes, depending on how soft you like the yolk. Using a slotted spoon, remove the egg from the water and drain it on a double layer of kitchen paper. Repeat the process with the other egg.

❹ Squeeze any excess moisture out of the spinach and spoon it on the cheese and ham topped muffins. Finally place a poached egg on each one. Season with black pepper and serve immediately.This is a delicious brunch dish for those special mid mornings when you have a little time on your hands.

(4) Fresh tomato pizzas

Takes 20 minutes

serves **2**   *POINTS* values per recipe **7.5**   calories per serving **245**   **V**

Another easy dish using English muffins for a quick and tasty pizza at brunchtime.

2 medium English muffins, split in half
1 teaspoon olive oil
½ small onion
1 tablespoon tomato purée
1 tablespoon burger relish
1 large beef steak tomato, sliced
1 teaspoon balsamic vinegar
15 g (½ oz) Parmesan, shaved
freshly ground black pepper
4 fresh basil leaves (optional)

❶ Toast the muffins lightly on both sides. Heat the olive oil in a small pan and cook the onion for a few minutes, just to soften.

❷ Mix together the tomato purée and burger relish and spread a little over each muffin half. Spoon over the cooked onions and then top with the tomato slices.

❸ Drizzle with a little balsamic vinegar, then top with Parmesan shavings and a grinding of fresh black pepper.

❹ Finally top with a basil leaf, if desired.

TOP TIP Use a potato peeler to shave thin slices of the Parmesan; it's easier than using a knife.

Pizza calzone

Takes 35 minutes + 1 hour rising

serves **2**   *POINTS* values per recipe **12**   calories per serving **399**   **V**

A calzone is a pizza that has been folded over to enclose the filling – rather like a giant Cornish pasty. If you've never tried making pizza dough before, do give it a go as it really is very simple, plus the kneading is a great way of working out any built up tension! Serve with a crisp 0 *POINTS* value mixed salad.

FOR THE PIZZA DOUGH
175 g (6 oz) plain flour, plus extra for kneading
1 teaspoon fast action yeast
½ teaspoon sugar
1 teaspoon olive oil
salt and freshly ground black pepper

FOR THE FILLING
100 g (3½ oz) Quark
2 teaspoons freshly grated Parmesan cheese
75 g (2¾ oz) pimientos preserved in brine, drained and sliced
1 tablespoon shredded fresh basil
3 tablespoons passata

❶ Sift the flour into a mixing bowl, then stir in the yeast, sugar and ½ teaspoon salt. Make a well in the centre, pour in the oil and add enough warm water to bring the dough together – about 125 ml (4 fl oz).

❷ Turn out on to a floured surface and knead for 3 minutes until smooth. Return to the bowl, cover with clingfilm and leave to rise for 1 hour, or until doubled in bulk.

❸ Preheat the oven to Gas Mark 6/200°C/fan oven 180°C.

❹ For the filling, mix the Quark and Parmesan together with some seasoning. Mix the pimientos, basil and passata together.

❺ Divide the dough ball in half and roll each out to an 18 cm (7 inch) circle. Transfer to a baking sheet.

❻ Spread the Quark mixture over half of each dough circle and top this with the pimiento mixture. Moisten the edges with water, fold the untopped dough over the filling and pinch the edges to seal. Make a small hole in the top of each calzone.

❼ Bake for 10–12 minutes until crisp and golden.

TOP TIPS Make double the quantity of pizza dough and roll out a 25 cm (10 inch) pizza base. Open freeze on a baking tray until firm then wrap well in clingfilm. Cook the base from frozen, adding an extra 3 minutes to the cooking time.

VARIATION For a meaty calzone, substitute dry fried mushrooms, cooked spinach and 60 g (2 oz) wafer thin ham for the Quark, Parmesan and pimientos. The *POINTS* values per serving will then be 5.

(3½ POINTS VALUE) Smoked haddock on potato pancakes

Takes 45 minutes

serves **2**   *POINTS* values per recipe **7.5**   calories per serving **300**

These fluffy pancakes make a satisfying brunch or supper dish.

2 smoked haddock fillets, weighing approximately 125 g (4½ oz) each
fresh parsley, to garnish (optional)
salt and freshly ground black pepper

FOR THE PANCAKES
250 g (9 oz) peeled potatoes, cut into chunks
25 g (1 oz) plain flour
50 ml (2 fl oz) hot skimmed milk
freshly grated nutmeg
2 egg whites
low fat cooking spray

FOR THE MUSTARD SAUCE
2 tablespoons half fat crème fraîche
1 teaspoon Dijon mustard

❶ Boil the potatoes in plenty of salted water for about 15 minutes until tender, then mash in a large bowl and leave to cool slightly.

❷ Mix in the flour, milk, seasoning and a little grated nutmeg. Whisk the egg whites until stiff then fold gently into the mixture.

❸ Heat a large frying pan and spray with the low fat cooking spray. Drop tablespoonfuls of the mixture into the pan and cook for 2–3 minutes, flip over with a palette knife and cook for another 2–3 minutes until golden. Set aside on a plate and keep warm while you cook the remaining mixture (making 10 pancakes altogether).

❹ Meanwhile, preheat the grill. Lay the haddock fillets on a piece of foil on the grill pan. Season and spray with the low fat cooking spray. Grill for 2–3 minutes on each side until cooked through.

❺ Make the sauce by stirring together all the ingredients.

❻ Divide the potato pancakes between two serving plates. Add a smoked haddock fillet and some of the sauce to each plate. Serve garnished with parsley sprigs, if using.

Potato and artichoke frittata

Takes 35 minutes

serves **4**   *POINTS* values per recipe **13**   calories per serving **230**   **V**

Any leftovers are delicious eaten cold the next day or packed into your lunchbox.

225 g (8 oz) potatoes, peeled and sliced thinly
1 tablespoon vegetable oil
1 red onion, sliced
425 g (15 oz) canned artichoke hearts, drained and quartered
5 eggs
5 tablespoons skimmed milk
½ teaspoon dried thyme
salt and freshly ground black pepper

❶ Bring a pan of lightly salted water to the boil and cook the potato slices for 5 minutes. Drain thoroughly.

❷ Meanwhile, heat the oil in a 20 cm (8 inch) non stick frying pan and add the onion. Cook for 5 minutes until softened. Add the cooked potato slices and artichoke hearts to the pan. Carefully toss with a wooden spatula so they are evenly distributed.

❸ Beat together the eggs, milk, thyme and seasoning and pour into the pan. Cook over a low heat for about 5 minutes until you see the edges beginning to set

❹ Transfer the pan to a moderate grill and cook the top for a further 2 to 3 minutes until set and golden. Leave to stand in the pan for 5 minutes, then carefully transfer to a serving plate and cut into wedges to serve.

TOP TIP Omelettes are the perfect way to use up leftover veggies; basically anything goes.

Summer vegetable omelette

Takes 25 minutes

serves **2**   *POINTS* values per recipe **6**   calories per serving **240**   **V**

A large, Spanish style, thick omelette that you can slice into wedges and eat hot or cold. Delicious served with a crispy 0 *POINTS* values cucumber and mint salad.

100 g (3½ oz) asparagus spears, sliced into rounds
200 g (7 oz) green beans, sliced into small rounds
4 eggs, beaten
a small bunch of coriander or thyme, chopped
a small bunch of parsley, chopped
a medium bunch of spring onions, chopped
4 tablespoons skimmed milk
low fat cooking spray
salt and freshly ground black pepper

❶ Blanch the asparagus and green beans in boiling, salted water for 2 minutes, drain, then place in a large bowl.

❷ Add the eggs, herbs, spring onions, milk and seasoning to the bowl and mix together. Heat a large, heavy based, non stick frying pan and spray with the low fat cooking spray.

❸ Pour in the egg mixture and reduce the heat to very low. Cook, without stirring, for 15–20 minutes or until the eggs have set and the base is golden brown (check by gently lifting the edge with a palette knife).

❹ Heat the grill to high and place the pan under it to quickly grill the top of the omelette – 2 minutes should be long enough, then slide it out of the pan on to a plate and serve cut in slices.

TOP TIP The secret of cooking the omelette through without burning is to cook on a very low heat and leave it for a long time.

4 POINTS VALUE Breakfast salad

Takes 30 minutes

serves **4**   *POINTS* values per recipe **16.5**   calories per serving **185**

This substantial salad is perfect for a brunch or lunchtime treat to stave off those hunger pangs.

225 g (8 oz) low fat sausages
150 g (5½ oz) lean back bacon
low fat cooking spray
225 g (8 oz) open cup mushrooms, sliced
225 g (8 oz) cherry tomatoes, halved
1 tablespoon wholegrain mustard
1 tablespoon dark soy sauce
1 teaspoon clear honey
350 g (12 oz) Iceberg lettuce, shredded

❶ Grill the sausages for about 10 minutes until evenly browned and cooked through, and grill the bacon until crispy. Slice the sausages into rings and chop the bacon into small pieces.

❷ Meanwhile, spray a frying pan with the low fat cooking spray and add the mushrooms. Cook them for 5 minutes until they are tender. Add the tomatoes, mustard, soy sauce and honey, and cook for a further 2 minutes, stirring occasionally. Add the sausages and bacon, and mix everything well.

❸ Divide the Iceberg lettuce between four serving plates and top with the 'breakfast' mix. Serve at once.

VARIATION For a vegetarian alternative, omit the bacon and use vegetarian sausages instead. The *POINTS* values per serving will be 2.

8 POINTS VALUE Light spaghetti carbonara

Takes 15 minutes

serves **1**   *POINTS* values per recipe **8**   calories per serving **490**

This popular, creamy bacon pasta sauce can often be extremely high in *POINTS* values. This recipe shows you how to make a lighter version that is just as tasty, but much healthier.

75 g (2½ oz) spaghetti
1 egg yolk
5 tablespoons semi skimmed milk
½ teaspoon cornflour
2 teaspoons grated Parmesan cheese
low fat cooking spray
1 rasher of lean smoked back bacon, trimmed of fat and cut into fine strips
1 garlic clove, chopped
salt and freshly ground black pepper

❶ Cook the spaghetti in lightly salted, boiling water according to the pack instructions. Drain the pasta, remove it from the pan and set it aside.

❷ Meanwhile, beat the egg yolk, milk, cornflour and 1 teaspoon of the Parmesan cheese together in a cup.

❸ Spray the same pasta pan with low fat cooking spray and stir fry the bacon strips and garlic for about 2 minutes. Return the pasta to the pan. Add seasoning and reheat the mixture, stirring, until it is piping hot.

(1) Apple drop scones

Takes 20 minutes + 15 minutes standing time

makes **18** *POINTS* values per recipe **21.5** calories per serving **65** V

These scones are ideal for a tea time treat and taste best when fresh and warm from the oven.

100 g (3½ oz) self raising flour
50 g (1¾ oz) Jordans Original Crunchy Cereal (Raisins & Almonds)
1 apple, peeled, cored and chopped finely
a pinch of salt
25 g (1 oz) golden caster sugar
1 large egg
150 ml (¼ pint) skimmed milk
2 teaspoons vegetable oil
9 teaspoons very low fat spread
18 teaspoons reduced sugar strawberry spread

❶ Put the flour, cereal, apple, salt and sugar into a large bowl. Add the egg and milk and beat well until all the ingredients are thoroughly combined. Cover and allow to stand for 15 minutes.

❷ Heat a large, heavy based frying pan or griddle until hot. Add a little oil, then drop tablespoons of the mixture into the hot pan. Cook until bubbles appear on the surface, then flip over to cook the other side.

❸ Transfer the cooked drop scones to kitchen paper to cool slightly. Continue to cook the remaining batter in the same way until it is all used.

❹ Serve each scone with ½ teaspoon of very low fat spread and a teaspoonful of strawberry spread.

(2½) Winter fruits with mango and vanilla whip

Takes 15 minutes

serves **4** *POINTS* values per recipe **9.5** calories per serving **155** V

Fresh fruit is so good for you, especially during the winter, when you might not eat so many salads and raw food. You need those vitamins! Remember to adjust the *POINTS* values as necessary in the variations below.

4 satsumas, clementines or mandarins, peeled and sliced
225 g (8 oz) red or green seedless grapes, halved
2 fresh figs, sliced thinly
1 banana, sliced
1 teaspoon of finely grated lime or lemon zest
2 tablespoons lime or lemon juice
1 small mango, peeled, stoned and chopped
150 g (5½ oz) low fat plain yogurt
1 teaspoon vanilla essence

❶ Put the satsumas, clementines or mandarins with the grapes, figs and banana into a large serving bowl. Add the lime or lemon zest and juice and toss together to mix.

❷ Put a few chunks of mango into the fruit salad, then put the remainder of the mango into a food processor or blender with the yogurt and vanilla essence. Blend together until smooth.

❸ Serve the fruit salad with the mango and vanilla sauce.

VARIATION 1 Use two large oranges instead of the satsumas, clementines or mandarins. Try using a large wedge of Charentais melon instead of the mango.

VARIATION 2 If you're not keen on figs, use a large peach or nectarine instead.

Griddle cakes with banana jam

Takes 35 minutes

makes **16**   *POINTS* values per recipe **23**   calories per serving **85**   **V**

100 g (3½ oz) self raising flour
a pinch of salt
1 egg
1 tablespoon treacle
150 ml (¼ pint) skimmed milk
15 g (½ oz) butter

FOR THE BANANA JAM
200 ml (7 fl oz) fresh apple juice
a cinnamon stick, broken in half
2 cloves
5 cm (2 inch) strip of pared lemon rind
1 tablespoon lemon juice
1 tablespoon dark muscovado sugar
4 medium ripe bananas
15 g (½ oz) butter

❶ First make the batter. Sift the flour and salt into a bowl. Make a well in the centre and break in the egg. Add the treacle and milk and work in the flour to make a smooth batter. Leave to stand for 10 minutes. Make the banana jam.

❷ Heat the fruit juice with the cinnamon, cloves, lemon rind, juice and sugar. Boil rapidly to reduce to 6 tablespoons. Strain into a bowl, add the bananas and mash to a smooth purée. Beat in the butter.

❸ Heat a heavy based frying pan and rub some of the butter over the surface. Use a ladle to pour on small mounds of batter, spacing well apart. As soon as the cakes are bubbling, turn them over with a palette knife and cook until set and golden brown on the other side. Keep the batches warm in a folded clean tea towel until all the mixture has been cooked. Serve the griddle cakes with the banana jam.

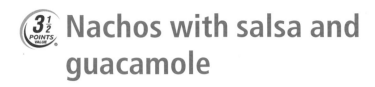

Nachos with salsa and guacamole

Takes 25 minutes

serves **4**   *POINTS* values per recipe **15**   calories per serving **237**   **V**

Quark keeps the *POINTS* values low in this delicious guacamole – with chips it makes a great snack to enjoy with friends at any time.

FOR THE TORTILLAS
4 x 20 cm (8 inch) flour tortillas
low fat cooking spray
1 teaspoon smoked paprika

FOR THE GUACAMOLE
450 g (1 lb) ripe tomatoes
1 avocado
100 g (3½ oz) Quark
1 red onion, chopped finely
juice of 1 lime
a few drops of Tabasco sauce

FOR THE SALSA
2 tablespoons of freshly chopped coriander
salt and freshly ground black pepper

❶ Preheat the oven to Gas Mark 4/180°C/fan oven 160°C. Spray the tortillas with low fat cooking spray and sprinkle lightly with the smoked paprika. Using kitchen scissors, cut each tortilla into four strips, and then into small triangles. Spread out on a baking tray and bake for 6–7 minutes until golden. Leave to cool and crisp up.

❷ To make the guacamole, cut a small cross in the base of each tomato then place in a bowl and cover with boiling water. Stand for 1 minute then drain and slip off the skins. Quarter and de-seed one tomato, then finely dice the flesh. Mash the avocado flesh with the Quark, then mix in the diced tomato, half the red onion and half the lime juice plus Tabasco and seasoning to taste.

❸ To make the salsa, roughly chop the rest of the tomatoes and mix with the coriander, the remaining lime juice and red onion, in a separate bowl.

❹ Serve the tortilla chips with the guacamole and salsa.

TOP TIP Smoked paprika, also known as pimentón, has a wonderfully rich smoky flavour, and is sold with the other spices in most major supermarkets. However, ordinary paprika can be used instead.

(2) Parsnip and lemon soup

Takes 10 minutes to prepare, 35 minutes to cook

serves **4**   *POINTS* values per recipe **7.5**   calories per serving **130**   ❄   V

Parsnips and lemons are a delicious combination for soup.

15 g (½ oz) polyunsaturated margarine
1 onion, chopped
450 g (1 lb) parsnips, peeled and chopped
½ teaspoon ground cumin
2 vegetable stock cubes, dissolved in 600 ml (1 pint) hot water
1 tablespoon chopped fresh parsley
300 ml (½ pint) skimmed milk
finely grated zest of 1 lemon
salt and freshly ground black pepper

TO GARNISH
parsley sprigs
lemon zest

❶ Melt the margarine in a large saucepan and sauté the onion until softened, about 5 minutes. Add the parsnips and cook, stirring, for another 2–3 minutes.

❷ Add the ground cumin, vegetable stock and chopped parsley. Bring to the boil, then reduce the heat and simmer gently for about 20 minutes, or until the parsnips are tender.

❸ Transfer the mixture to a food processor or blender and liquidise until smooth. Return to the saucepan and add the milk and lemon zest. Reheat gently. Season to taste.

❹ Ladle the soup into warmed bowls, then garnish with parsley sprigs and lemon zest.

VARIATION 1 Try using fresh coriander in the recipe instead of parsley, for a change.

VARIATION 2 Orange zest also tastes delicious with parsnips, so try it instead of lemon zest.

 # Gazpacho

Takes 20 minutes + 3–4 hours chilling

serves **6**   *POINTS* values per recipe **1**   calories per serving **50**   ❄ **V**

Serve this tomato based, chilled Spanish soup in the summer as a cool and refreshing 0 *POINTS* values starter.

1 bunch of spring onions, chopped roughly

4 ripe tomatoes, peeled and chopped roughly

½ cucumber, chopped roughly

1 small green pepper, de-seeded and chopped roughly

1 garlic clove, crushed

2 tablespoons chopped fresh flat leaf parsley or mint

400 g can of chopped tomatoes

300 ml (10 fl oz) tomato juice, chilled

3 tablespoons red wine vinegar

1 teaspoon caster sugar

300 ml (10 fl oz) chilled water

salt and freshly ground black pepper

1 tablespoon each of finely chopped red onion, cucumber, red pepper and tomatoes, to garnish

❶ Place all the ingredients, apart from the garnishes, in a blender or food processor and liquidise until smooth. Do this in batches, if necessary.

❷ Strain the soup through a sieve, using the back of a wooden spoon to push it through, extracting as much liquid as possible from the ingredients. Cover and chill until icy cold for 3–4 hours, or overnight if preferred.

❸ Taste the soup and check the seasoning, adding salt and pepper according to taste. Ladle the soup into six bowls and top with the garnishes.

TOP TIP An easy way to peel tomatoes is to put them into a bowl and cover them with boiling water. Leave for 15–20 seconds, and then remove from the water and slip off their skins.

VARIATION If you're not keen on peppers, leave them out and use another two tomatoes instead.

(5) Mexican beanburgers

Takes 20 minutes + 30 minutes chilling

serves **4**   *POINTS* values per recipe **20.5**   calories per serving **370**   ❄   **V**

These spicy Mexican style beanburgers have a really satisfying texture and give a gentle kick! Serve with relish and a big green salad for no extra *POINTS* values.

2 x 400 g cans of mixed beans, rinsed and drained
1 small onion, chopped roughly
1 garlic clove, chopped
400 g can of mixed peppers in brine, rinsed, drained and chopped roughly
1 medium red chilli, de-seeded and chopped finely
1 teaspoon ground cumin seeds
2 tablespoons Worcestershire sauce
1 tablespoon tomato purée, diluted with 1 tablespoon water
a small bunch of fresh parsley, coriander or chives
1 egg, beaten
2 tablespoons plain white flour
low fat cooking spray
4 medium burger buns
salt and freshly ground black pepper
salad leaves of your choice, to serve

❶ Put all the ingredients except the flour and cooking spray in a food processor and whizz to a rough paste. Shape the mixture into four burgers, put the flour on a plate and coat the burgers in it. Refrigerate for 30 minutes to allow them to firm up.

❷ Heat a large frying pan and spray with the low fat cooking spray then fry the burgers for about 4 minutes on each side until browned and heated through.

❸ Split the buns and fill with the burgers and salad leaves, then serve.

Curried root veg and couscous lunch pot

Takes 35 minutes to prepare, 20 minutes to cook

serves **4**   *POINTS* values per recipe **16.5**   calories per serving **355**   ❄   **V**

Pack into pots for a healthy lunchtime treat.

225 g (8 oz) couscous
finely grated zest of one lemon
300 ml (½ pint) boiling water
1 tablespoon olive oil
1 onion, sliced
225 g (8 oz) carrots, peeled and sliced
350 g (12oz) swede, peeled and diced
225 g (8 oz) parsnips, peeled and sliced
1 tablespoon medium curry powder
¼ teaspoon ground cinnamon
400 g (14 oz) canned chopped tomatoes
150 ml (¼ pint) vegetable stock
2 tablespoons chopped fresh coriander
salt and freshly ground black pepper

❶ Place the couscous and lemon zest in a bowl and pour the boiling water over. Fluff the couscous up with a fork, cover the bowl with a clean tea towel. Leave to stand for 10 minutes, fluffing it up from time to time.

❷ Meanwhile, heat the oil in the pan and cook the onion, carrots, swede and parsnips for 5 minutes. Stir in the curry powder and cinnamon and cook for a further 2 minutes.

❸ Add the chopped tomatoes, stock and seasoning and bring to the boil. Cover and simmer for 20 minutes, until the vegetables are tender. Remove the lid, raise the heat and allow the juices to bubble and evaporate into a thick sauce.

❹ Combine the couscous with the vegetable mixture, seasoning and coriander. Eat hot or allow to cool and chill until required.

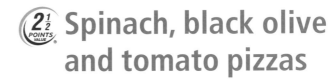

Spinach, black olive and tomato pizzas

Takes 20 minutes

serves **4**   *POINTS* values per recipe **9.5**   calories per serving **235**   **V**

2 English muffins, halved
2 tablespoons sun dried tomato paste
½ teaspoon dried mixed herbs
150 g (5½ oz) baby spinach
1 beefsteak tomato, sliced
25 g (1 oz) pitted black olives, halved
50 g (1¾ oz) reduced fat mozzarella cheese, sliced thinly
salt and freshly ground black pepper

❶ Lightly toast the muffin halves on both sides. Mix together the tomato paste and mixed herbs. Spread on to one side of each muffin half.

❷ Rinse the spinach and place in a pan. Cover tightly and cook for 2 minutes until wilted. Drain, squeezing out any excess moisture and arrange on top of the pizza with a slice of tomato, a few olive halves and sliced mozzarella.

❸ Season well and return to the grill for 2 to 3 minutes until the cheese has melted.

Fiery chicken pitta pockets

5½ POINTS VALUE

Takes 30 minutes + 1 hour marinating

serves **4**   **POINTS** values per recipe **22**   calories per serving **340**   ❄

Spice up some chicken breasts, then serve in pitta bread with chopped fresh salad and a good squeeze of lime juice. Children will love this if they like spicy things. If you don't have time to marinate the chicken, use the mixture for basting.

2 teaspoons olive oil
1 tablespoon paprika
1 teaspoon mild chilli powder
2 teaspoons finely grated fresh root ginger
3 tablespoons lime or lemon juice
1 tablespoon chopped fresh coriander or mint
4 medium skinless, boneless chicken breasts
4 medium pitta breads
salt and freshly ground black pepper

TO SERVE
salad leaves, shredded
chopped cucumber, radish and tomato
sprigs of fresh coriander or mint
lime or lemon wedges

❶ In a shallow glass or plastic bowl, mix together the olive oil, paprika, chilli powder, ginger, lime or lemon juice and chopped herbs. Season with salt and pepper.

❷ Lay the chicken breasts in the mixture. Cover and leave to marinate for about 1 hour.

❸ Preheat the grill, then cook the chicken for about 12–15 minutes, turning once and basting often, until tender. When tested with a fork, the juices should run clear.

❹ Warm the pitta breads, either by wrapping in foil and heating under the grill, or by toasting lightly.

❺ Slice the chicken and serve in the warm pitta bread with shredded salad leaves, cucumber, radish and tomato. Garnish with fresh coriander or mint and serve with lime or lemon wedges.

(6½ POINTS VALUE) Creamy chicken pasta

Takes 35 minutes

serves **4**   *POINTS* values per recipe **25.5**   calories per serving **420**

Try this delicious pasta dish for a quick and simple supper.

1 tablespoon plain flour
2 medium skinless, boneless chicken breasts, cut into chunks
2 tablespoons olive oil
225 g (8 oz) tagliatelle
100 g (3½ oz) mange tout peas, sliced
1 courgette, chopped
300 ml (½ pint) skimmed milk
1 chicken or vegetable stock cube
1 teaspoon mixed dried Italian herbs
2 tomatoes, skinned and chopped finely
1 tablespoon finely grated Parmesan cheese
salt and freshly ground black pepper
basil sprigs, to garnish

❶ Sprinkle the flour on to a plate and season with salt and pepper. Roll the chicken pieces in this mixture.

❷ Heat the olive oil in a large frying pan and add the chicken pieces. Cook for about 6–8 minutes, turning often, until brown.

❸ Meanwhile, cook the tagliatelle in a large saucepan of lightly salted boiling water for about 8 minutes, until tender. At the same time, cook the mange tout peas with the courgette in a little lightly salted water for about 5 minutes.

❹ Add the milk, stock cube and mixed herbs to the chicken and stir until just boiling. Reduce the heat and cook gently for 2–3 minutes, stirring often.

❺ Drain the tagliatelle and the vegetables and toss them together with the tomatoes. Add the chicken mixture and stir together gently. Season to taste, then serve, sprinkled with Parmesan cheese and garnished with basil.

VARIATION 1 Use your choice of pasta shapes instead of tagliatelle, and use shaves of Parmesan cheese instead of grated.

VARIATION 2 For a vegetarian version, use 225 g (8 oz) of smoked tofu pieces instead of chicken. The *POINTS* values will be 5½ per serving.

 # Summer pasta

Takes 30 minutes

serves **2**   *POINTS* values per recipe **8.5**   calories per serving **320**

Fresh peas and mint put you in mind of summer – try this recipe to get you in the mood!

100 g (3½ oz) penne pasta
3 tablespoons frozen or fresh peas
100 g (3½ oz) mange tout peas, shredded
1 bunch of fresh mint, leaves only, chopped
low fat cooking spray
100 g (3½ oz) ham, cut into strips
1 teaspoon olive oil
salt and freshly ground black pepper

❶ Cook the pasta in a medium saucepan of lightly salted, boiling water for 10–12 minutes.

❷ Meanwhile bring a small saucepan of water to the boil and add the peas, mange tout peas and half the mint. Cook for 3–4 minutes. Drain and set aside.

❸ Spray a small frying pan with low fat cooking spray and cook the ham, turning occasionally, until it is golden.

❹ When the pasta is cooked, drain and return it to the pan. Add the cooked peas, mint, mange tout peas, ham and olive oil. Shred or chop the remaining mint and add this to the pan. Check the seasoning and serve immediately.

 Tropical crab and fruit salad

Takes 5 minutes

serves **4**   *POINTS* values per recipe **12.5**   calories per serving **205**

This recipe is based on a South East Asian salad and is delicious.

240 g (8½ oz) fresh crab meat or 2 x 120 g cans of white crabmeat, drained
1 cucumber, grated
8 small pink radishes, halved and sliced thinly
2 ripe mangos or papayas, peeled and sliced
2 teaspoons caster sugar
1½ teaspoons fish or soy sauce
1 teaspoon crushed dried chilli
juice of 2 limes
1 small red chilli, de-seeded and chopped
50 g (1¾ oz) roasted peanuts, chopped
a small bunch of chives or coriander, chopped
salt

❶ Put all the ingredients except the chilli, peanuts and chives or coriander in a bowl and toss together gently. Pile on to serving plates, then sprinkle with the chilli, nuts and chives or coriander and serve.

 Lamb's lettuce niçoise

Takes 15 minutes

serves **4**   *POINTS* values per recipe **12.5**   calories per serving **230**

150 g (5½ oz) fine green beans
2 tablespoons olive oil
1 teaspoon finely grated lemon zest
1 tablespoon lemon juice
1 teaspoon Dijon or wholegrain mustard
1 tablespoon white wine or rice vinegar
4 generous handfuls of lamb's lettuce
4 tomatoes, cut into wedges
20 pitted black olives
4 small eggs, hard boiled and quartered
185 g can of tuna chunks in water or brine, drained
salt and freshly ground black pepper
chopped fresh parsley, to garnish

❶ Cook the beans in lightly salted boiling water until just tender – about 5 minutes.

❷ While the beans are cooking, make up the dressing by whisking together the olive oil, lemon zest and juice, mustard and vinegar. Season with a little salt and pepper.

❸ Drain the beans and add the dressing, tossing to coat. Allow to cool for a few minutes.

❹ Meanwhile, arrange the lamb's lettuce and tomatoes on four serving plates. Divide the warm beans between them, then top each salad with 5 olives, 1 egg and an equal amount of tuna. Sprinkle with parsley, then serve.

VARIATION If you're not keen on olives, simply leave them out. The *POINTS* values per serving will be the same.

④ Pasta pomodoro

POINTS VALUE

Takes 25 minutes

serves **4**   *POINTS* values per recipe **16**   calories per serving **330**   **V**

Use some ready made pasta sauce with a few other ingredients to make a quick and easy meal.

225 g (8 oz) pasta shapes
1 tablespoon olive oil
1 onion, chopped finely
100 g (3½ oz) mushrooms, wiped and sliced
400 g (14 oz) canned chopped tomatoes
275 g jar of tomato pasta sauce
100 g (3½ oz) roasted pepper strips in olive oil, rinsed and drained
salt and freshly ground black pepper
a handful of basil leaves, torn into pieces, to garnish

❶ Cook the pasta in plenty of lightly salted boiling water for 8–10 minutes until tender, or follow the pack instructions.

❷ Meanwhile, heat the olive oil in a large saucepan and sauté the onion for about 3 minutes, until softened.

❸ Add the mushrooms, canned tomatoes and pasta sauce. Bring up to the boil, then reduce the heat and simmer without a lid for about 10 minutes.

❹ Drain the pasta and add to the sauce with the pepper strips. Season to taste with salt and pepper, then serve, garnished with the torn basil leaves.

TOP TIP Instead of using pepper strips in olive oil, buy a can of red peppers and slice the amount you need. Keep the remainder in a covered container in the fridge, and use within 3 days.

2½ Sun drenched turkey towers

POINTS VALUE

Takes 40 minutes

serves **4**   *POINTS* values per recipe **10**   calories per serving **205**

You really need a griddle pan or BBQ to make these.

4 turkey breast steaks, weighing approximately 100 g (3½ oz) each,
   sliced into four even sized medallions
juice and zest of 1 lemon
1 garlic clove, crushed
1 teaspoon olive oil
2 aubergines, cut into 16 slices, about 5 mm (¼ inch) thick
4 large beef tomatoes, cut into 16 slices, about 5 mm (¼ inch) thick
2 tablespoons pesto sauce, mixed with 2 tablespoons boiling water
2 yellow peppers, quartered and de-seeded
salt and freshly ground black pepper
fresh basil, chopped, to garnish

❶ Put the turkey steaks on a large plate and season. Mix together the lemon juice, garlic and olive oil and pour over the turkey.

❷ Preheat a griddle pan so it's really hot. Brush the aubergine and tomato slices with the pesto sauce. Char the turkey steaks on both sides on the griddle and then turn down the heat and cook them for about 2 minutes more, until cooked through. Remove from the heat and set aside but keep warm.

❸ Get the griddle really hot again and then char all the vegetables on both sides, brushing with more pesto sauce as you go. As they are done, remove from the heat and set aside but keep warm.

❹ To serve, place a slice of aubergine on each plate then top with a piece of turkey, a slice of tomato and a slice of pepper. Repeat the layers to make a tower and serve two towers on each plate, scattered with basil.

Tomato, courgette and Parmesan tarts

5½ POINTS VALUE

Takes 30 minutes

serves **4**   *POINTS* values per recipe **22.5**   calories per serving **220**   **V**

One bite of these crispy tarts with their blend of tomato, courgette and Parmesan cheese whisks you off to the shores of the Mediterranean! Accompany them with a tossed mixed salad for a perfect summer lunch.

1 sheet of ready rolled puff pastry
1 large courgette, cut into 5 mm (¼ inch) thick slices
1 teaspoon olive oil
4 tomatoes, sliced thinly
25 g (1 oz) freshly grated Parmesan cheese
salt and freshly ground black pepper

1 Preheat the oven to Gas Mark 7/220°C/fan oven 200°C. Using a 10 cm (4 inch) saucer as a template, cut out four discs of pastry and place them on a heavy non stick baking sheet. Prick the pastry well.

2 Place another heavy non stick baking sheet on top and bake for 12–15 minutes until the pastry discs are pale golden, crisp and flat. Remove the top baking sheet.

3 Meanwhile, preheat the grill. Brush one side of the courgette slices with the oil. Arrange them on a baking sheet, oiled side up, and grill them under a high heat for about 5 minutes just on one side, until they are softened.

4 Lay the courgette slices on the four pastry discs. Place the tomato slices on top, arranged so the slices overlap each other. You can pile the slices high because they shrink while cooking. Season well with salt and pepper, and sprinkle over the Parmesan.

5 Return the tarts to the oven for another 5 minutes or so, until the cheese just melts. Cool slightly before serving.

VARIATION You can make these tarts even lower in *POINTS* values by substituting four wholemeal bread slices, lightly toasted, for the pastry discs. The *POINTS* values will be 2 per serving.

(2) Filo cups with apricot cream

Takes 30 minutes

serves **4**   **POINTS** values per recipe **9**   calories per serving **140**   **V**

These little pastries are heavenly – the melt in the mouth filo pastry contrasts perfectly with the tangy creamy filling…delicious!

1 teaspoon icing sugar
2 tablespoons low fat spread, melted
4 x 30 cm x 17 cm (12 inch x 6½ inch) sheets of filo pastry
420 g can of apricots in natural juice, drained
200 g (7 oz) very low fat plain fromage frais
artificial sweetener (optional)
ground cinnamon, to serve

❶ Mix the icing sugar with the melted low fat spread. With a pastry brush, dab this mixture over each filo sheet, and then cut each one into quarters. Layer the quartered sheets into four bun tins, placing them at angles to each other to form the cups.

❷ Heat the oven to Gas Mark 5/190°C/fan oven 170°C. Bake the filo cups for 10–12 minutes until they are golden brown and crisp. Cool them until required.

❸ Pat the apricots dry with kitchen paper and then chop them finely. Mix the apricot pieces with the fromage frais – add sweetener to the mixture if you like. Chill the apricot cream until ready to serve.

❹ Spoon the apricot cream into the cups, dust with cinnamon and serve.

VARIATION Try a 400 g (14 oz) punnet of fresh ripe strawberries instead of apricots. Crush with a fork until mushy but not too runny. Omit the cinnamon but stir ½ teaspoon vanilla essence into the fromage frais. The **POINTS** values will remain the same.

(2) Orange semolina puddings

Takes 20 minutes + cooling time

serves **4**   **POINTS** values per recipe **8.5**   calories per serving **135**   **V**

Semolina takes on a more sophisticated slant with these lovely light puddings.

25 g (1 oz) semolina
450 ml (16 fl oz) skimmed milk
powdered sweetener, to taste
finely grated zest and segments of 1 large orange
2 eggs, separated
1 tablespoon caster sugar

❶ Preheat the oven to Gas Mark 5/190°C/fan oven 170°C.

❷ Put the semolina into a saucepan and stir in the milk. Bring up to the boil, stirring constantly until thickened. Reduce the heat and cook gently for 2–3 minutes.

❸ Remove from the heat, cool for a few minutes, then add sweetener to taste. Stir in the orange zest and egg yolks. Divide between four individual heatproof dishes or ramekins. Top with the orange segments.

❹ Beat the egg whites in a grease free bowl until they hold their shape. Whisk in the sugar, then pile on top of the desserts. Bake for 3–4 minutes until golden brown. Serve at once.

TOP TIP Use heat resistant glass or china teacups if you don't have individual pudding dishes – their saucers make handy serving plates too.

 # Hot toffee apples

Takes 15 minutes

serves **4**	**POINTS** values per recipe **9**	calories per serving **135**	V

Give in to temptation with this wonderfully tasty and sticky low **POINTS** values pudding.

3 tablespoons toffee flavoured ice cream syrup
2 large, unpeeled dessert apples, sliced thinly
500 g tub of fruit flavoured low fat yogurt (e.g. strawberry flavoured)

❶ Heat the toffee syrup in a frying pan and toss in the apple slices. Cook for 3 minutes, stirring gently.

❷ Divide the yogurt between four serving bowls and spoon the hot apples on top to serve.

VARIATION 1 This is also good with bananas or pears. The **POINTS** values will remain the same.

VARIATION 2 Try using natural maple syrup instead of toffee ice cream syrup – delicious! The **POINTS** values remain the same.

Mango maple yogurt ice

Takes 20 minutes + 4–6 hours freezing

serves **4**	**POINTS** values per recipe **11**	calories per serving **170**	V

This refreshing yogurt ice is guaranteed to cool you down on hot summer days.

450 g (1 lb) mangoes, peeled, stoned and sliced
3 tablespoons maple syrup
finely grated zest and juice of 1 lime
600 ml (20 fl oz) low fat plain yogurt

❶ Place the sliced mangoes in a food processor with the maple syrup, lime zest and juice and yogurt. Blend for about 30 seconds, until the mixture is smooth.

❷ Transfer the mixture to a freezer container with a tight filling lid and freeze for 2 hours. Remove from the freezer and whisk well to break down the ice crystals. Freeze for another hour and then whisk again.

❸ Repeat this two or three times more before the mixture freezes completely.

TOP TIP The more times you can whisk the yogurt ice while it is freezing, the smoother it will be.

 # Berried treasure

Takes 15 minutes

serves **4**   *POINTS* values per recipe **11.5**   calories per serving **190**   V

Make the most of summer berries in this fruity pudding. You could substitute thawed frozen berries when fresh ones are out of season.

225 g (8 oz) strawberries, hulled and sliced
225 g (8 oz) raspberries
100 g (3½ oz) blueberries
2 tablespoons crème de cassis or low sugar blackcurrant cordial
1 tablespoon caster sugar
1 tablespoon polyunsaturated margarine
50 g (1¾ oz) Jordans Original Crunchy (Raisins and Almonds)
25 g (1 oz) marzipan, grated

❶ Put the strawberries, raspberries and blueberries into a saucepan. Add the crème de cassis or blackcurrant cordial and sugar, stirring to mix. Heat gently for about 2 or 3 minutes.

❷ Divide the mixture between four individual heatproof dishes such as ramekins or heatproof teacups.

❸ Melt the margarine and add the cereal, breaking up any large clusters. Stir to coat, then sprinkle evenly over the fruit. Top with the grated marzipan.

❹ Preheat the grill. Grill the desserts until the marzipan turns golden brown, taking care as it can soon burn. Cool slightly, then serve.

TOP TIP Crème de cassis is a blackcurrant liqueur. However if you don't want to buy some just for this recipe, simply substitute a low sugar blackcurrant cordial instead.

VARIATION: You could also use 25 g (1 oz) ground almonds as a topping. Add in step 3 with the cereal, and grill the topping until golden brown. The *POINTS* values per serving will be 3½.

 # Little chocolate pots

Takes 20 minutes + 30 minutes chilling

serves **4**   *POINTS* values per recipe **14.5**   calories per serving **180**   V

These are very light and fluffy mousses that look great served in espresso cups or little pots.

2 eggs, separated
50 g (1¾ oz) caster sugar
50 g (1¾ oz) plain chocolate (70% cocoa solids), broken into pieces
150 ml (5 fl oz) 0% fat Greek style plain yogurt

❶ Put the egg yolks and sugar into a bowl and whisk with an electric whisk or by hand with a balloon whisk, until really thick and mousse like.

❷ Melt the chocolate in a bowl set over a pan of simmering water. Remove from the heat and allow to cool slightly, then whisk into the egg mixture.

❸ Fold the yogurt into the chocolate mixture until smooth. Whisk the egg whites until stiff then gently fold into the mixture.

❹ Spoon into four little cups or pots and refrigerate for about 30 minutes, until chilled and set.

 # Fruits of the forest cream

Takes 15 minutes

| serves **4** | ***POINTS*** values per recipe **4** | calories per serving **80** | | **V** |

This creamy, fruity dish is full of the flavours of summer.

250 g pack of ripe strawberries, hulled
125 g (4½ oz) blueberries or blackberries
125 g (4½ oz) raspberries
200 g tub of Quark
1 tablespoon artificial sweetener or to taste
4 mint sprigs for decoration

❶ In a big bowl, crush the strawberries with the other fruits using a fork or the back of a ladle. Reserve 4 teaspoons of crushed fruit for decoration.

❷ Add the Quark and stir until smooth. Add the sweetener to taste.

❸ Spoon the mixture into four serving bowls and top with the reserved crushed fruit and the mint.

VARIATION Try using very low fat fromage frais instead of Quark and add a little grated lemon zest. The ***POINTS*** values will remain the same.

Takes 15 minutes

serves **1** | *POINTS* values per recipe **5.5** | calories per serving **454**

Many people associate Japanese food with sushi and raw fish but there's a huge variety of less daunting cooked dishes as well. This seared salmon noodle bowl is an excellent example of Japan's delicate and refined cuisine.

FOR THE MARINADE
2 tablespoons teriyaki sauce
1 teaspoon granulated sweetener
juice of ½ a lime

FOR THE SALMON AND NOODLES
125 g (4½ oz) salmon fillet, skinned
30 g (1¼ oz) thin rice noodles
425 ml (15 fl oz) fish or chicken stock
60 g (2 oz) sugar snap peas, sliced
60 g (2 oz) beansprouts, rinsed
40 g (1½ oz) drained bamboo shoots
1 tablespoon chopped fresh coriander
½ red chilli, de-seeded and sliced
2 spring onions, sliced
wedge of lime, to serve

❶ Mix the teriyaki sauce, granulated sweetener and lime juice together in a dish. Turn the salmon in the marinade to coat and set aside while you prepare the other ingredients.

❷ Soak the rice noodles in boiling water for 5 minutes or according to pack instructions, then drain.

❸ Heat a non stick frying pan. Lift the salmon out of its marinade (reserving the marinade) then dry fry for 2½ minutes on each side until the flesh is richly caramelised.

❹ Meanwhile, bring the stock to the boil, add the reserved marinade and sugar snap peas and simmer for 3 minutes until just tender.

❺ Place the noodles in a deep bowl. Top with the beansprouts and bamboo shoots. Pour the hot broth and sugar snaps into the bowl and scatter with the coriander, chilli and spring onions. Place the seared salmon on top of the noodles. Serve with a wedge of lime to squeeze over.

VARIATION 1 The salmon can be replaced with a 125 g (4½ oz) skinless chicken breasts but remember it will need about 10 minutes to cook through.

VARIATION 2 The salmon can also be replaced with a 150 g (5½ oz) pork tenderloin. Cook for 10 minutes.

The *POINTS* values will be 3½ per serving for chicken and 4½ for pork.

Sweetcorn risotto

Takes 30 minutes

| serves **1** | *POINTS* values per recipe **7.5** | calories per serving **575** | V |

Risotto made with Arborio rice makes a wonderful one pot meal – tasty and very satisfying. The preparation is simple and of course, there is only one saucepan to wash up!

low fat cooking spray
1 small red onion, chopped
1 large garlic clove, chopped
75 g (2¾ oz) Arborio rice
350 ml (12 fl oz) boiling vegetable or chicken stock
170 g can of sweetcorn, drained and liquid reserved
1 tablespoon chopped fresh parsley
1 tablespoon grated Parmesan cheese
salt and freshly ground black pepper

❶ Heat a medium size saucepan and spray it with low fat cooking spray. Cook the onion and garlic with 2 tablespoons of water until they sizzle. Cover and cook for 5 minutes.

❷ Remove the cover, stir in the rice and cook for 1 minute. Stir in a quarter of the hot stock and season. Bring the pan to the boil and cook, stirring, until the stock is absorbed.

❸ Add another quarter of stock and stir until it is absorbed. Repeat this process twice more until all the stock is used up. This should take about 15 minutes.

❹ Stir in the sweetcorn and the reserved liquid, and bring the pan to the boil. Add the parsley and half the Parmesan cheese. Check the seasoning, and serve the risotto hot, sprinkled with the remaining cheese.

TOP TIP 1 To make the risotto ahead of time, par cook it for 10 minutes, using half the stock, and then cool it. Finish by reheating the remaining stock and continuing the recipe.

TOP TIP 2 Use proper risotto rice (Arborio or Carnaroli) for risottos. No other kind will give you that creaminess that makes risottos so delicious.

Moules Provençales

Takes 10 minutes

| serves **1** | **POINTS** values per recipe **3** | calories per serving **294** |

Mussels in their shells are very easy and quick to cook, and because they take longer to eat they seem very filling! This tomato based sauce is full of the flavours of the Mediterranean, so make sure you've got a spoon ready to scoop up all the goodness! Serve with a medium crusty bread roll for an extra 2 **POINTS** values.

1 teaspoon olive oil
1 small onion, chopped finely
1 celery stick, sliced
1 small courgette, diced
1 garlic clove, sliced
230 g can of chopped tomatoes with herbs
500 g (1 lb 2 oz) cleaned mussels (see top tip)
salt and freshly ground black pepper

❶ Heat the olive oil in a large saucepan, add the onion and cook for 2 minutes, then add the celery, courgette and garlic and cook for a further 2 minutes.

❷ Add the tinned tomatoes, 3 tablespoons of water, the mussels and some seasoning. Toss the mussels around in the sauce then cover the pan and cook for 5 minutes over a moderate heat, shaking the pan a couple of times until the mussels have opened. Discard any mussels that stay closed after cooking.

❸ Tip into a deep warmed bowl to serve and have another bowl ready to put the empty shells in as you eat.

TOP TIP To clean mussels, scrub them in a sinkful of cold water and pull away the thread-like 'beard'. Discard any mussels that don't close when given a sharp tap or that don't open during cooking.

 # Sweet and sour pork

Takes 40 minutes

serves **1**	*POINTS* values per recipe **4.5**	calories per serving **380**	❄

When you choose this popular dish at a Chinese restaurant or have it as a take away, you're likely to be using lots of *POINTS* values. It's much better to enjoy this home made version, which has all the flavour but few of the *POINTS* values.

1 teaspoon cornflour

1–2 teaspoons chilli sauce

1 teaspoon light or dark muscovado sugar

2 teaspoons rice or white wine vinegar

1 tablespoon light soy sauce

low fat cooking spray

100 g (3½ oz) lean pork shoulder, cut into strips

1 small garlic clove, crushed

1 small onion, sliced

1 small carrot, cut into fine strips

25 g (1 oz) mange tout peas, sliced

½ chicken or vegetable stock cube, dissolved in 100 ml (3½ fl oz) boiling water

1 tomato, skinned and quartered

salt and freshly ground black pepper

TO SERVE

75 g (2¾ oz) hot, cooked long grain rice

coriander sprigs or finely chopped spring onions (optional)

❶ In a small jug or bowl, mix together the cornflour, chilli sauce, sugar, vinegar and soy sauce.

❷ Heat a wok or large frying pan and lightly spray it with low fat cooking spray. Add the pork, stir frying it over a high heat for 3–4 minutes to seal and brown it.

❸ Add the garlic, onion, carrot and mange tout peas and stir fry for 2 minutes. Pour in the stock and bring to the boil. Reduce the heat and simmer gently for 15–20 minutes, or until the pork is tender.

❹ Mix in the tomato. Then add the blended cornflour mixture, stirring as you do so. Cook for 2 minutes, until the sauce is thickened. Check the seasoning, adding salt and pepper to taste.

❺ Serve in a bowl with the hot, cooked rice, garnished with coriander sprigs or finely chopped spring onions, if using.

VARIATION For a vegetarian version, use 100 g (3½ oz) Quorn cubes instead of the pork, and marinate them in the cornflour mixture for 20–30 minutes before you start to cook. Add them after the tomatoes in step 4 and remember to use a vegetable stock cube. The POINTS values per serving will be 3½.

Braised spicy beancurd

Takes 15 minutes

serves 1	POINTS values per recipe 1	calories per serving 105	V

A lively vegetarian dish with lots of flavour and hardly any POINTS values.

25 g (1 oz) mange tout
40 g (1½ oz) baby sweetcorn
low fat cooking spray
60 g (2 oz) beancurd, cubed
½ green pepper, de-seeded and sliced
½ teaspoon peeled and chopped fresh root ginger
1 garlic clove, crushed
1 tablespoon yellow bean sauce

❶ Steam the mange tout and baby sweetcorn for 6–8 minutes, until cooked but still crisp.

❷ Meanwhile, heat a small frying pan and spray with low fat cooking spray. Put in the beancurd, green pepper, ginger and garlic. Stir fry for 3–4 minutes, until the beancurd is golden.

❸ Add the yellow bean sauce and 3 tablespoons of water and stir whilst it bubbles and thickens.

❹ Serve the beancurd with the steamed vegetables.

VARIATION This recipe can be used for spicy prawns – omit the beancurd and replace with 60 g (2 oz) of raw prawns. The POINTS values will then be 1½ per serving.

(6) Steak au poivre

Takes 15 minutes

| serves **1** | **POINTS** values per recipe **6** | calories per serving **235** |

Treat yourself to a juicy fillet steak with lots of 0 **POINTS** value vegetables for a filling and delicious meal.

1 rounded teaspoon black or green peppercorns
100 g (3½ oz) fillet steak, trimmed
low fat cooking spray
1 tablespoon brandy
2 tablespoons half fat crème fraîche
Maldon salt or sea salt

TO SERVE
0 **POINTS** values vegetables, such as courgettes, mange tout peas and cauliflower
chopped fresh parsley (optional)

❶ Crush the peppercorns coarsely, either by using a mortar and pestle or a rolling pin.

❷ Press both sides of the fillet steak firmly on to the crushed peppercorns.

❸ Heat a heavy based frying pan and lightly spray it with low fat cooking spray. Over a high heat, add the steak and allow it to sear and brown for about 30 seconds. Turn it over and sear it on the other side. Reduce the heat to medium hot, and cook the steak for another 2–5 minutes on each side, or until cooked to your liking. Transfer to a warm serving plate, season with salt and keep warm.

❹ Add the brandy to the pan and let it bubble up for a few moments. Spoon in the crème fraîche, heat for about 30 seconds, and then pour this sauce over the steak.

❺ Serve with some 0 **POINTS** value vegetables and garnish with the parsley, if desired.

TOP TIP 1 Use sirloin or rump steak instead of fillet if you prefer the flavour. The **POINTS** values per serving will be 6 and 5½ respectively.

TOP TIP 2 A small helping of low fat oven baked chips will add a further 2 **POINTS** values to your meal.

 **Chinese steamed chicken**

Takes 25 minutes

| serves **1** | *POINTS* values per recipe **2** | calories per serving **160** | |

This dish uses the Chinese method of steaming which is ideal for producing a fast and tasty meal – the steaming juices making a delicious, tangy sauce for the chicken. Serve this with zero *POINTS* values, colourful vegetables that you have also steamed, and arrange them around the chicken. If you are feeling hungry you could have this with 150 g (51/2 oz) plain boiled rice, adding an extra 3 *POINTS* values.

100 g (3½ oz) skinless, boneless chicken breast
1 tablespoon light soy sauce
2 teaspoons dry sherry
1 pak choi (Chinese cabbage), halved or 50 g (1¾ oz) fresh Chinese leaf, shredded
a good pinch of Chinese five spice powder
½ teaspoon sesame oil
1 spring onion, sliced into long thin strips
salt and freshly ground black pepper

❶ With a sharp knife, slash the chicken breast twice on each side. Toss it in a polythene food bag with the soy sauce and sherry, and then set aside to marinate for 5 minutes.

❷ Meanwhile, place some water in the base of a saucepan and put it on the hob to boil. Place a metal or traditional bamboo steamer basket on top.

❸ Lay the pak choi or Chinese leaf on a heatproof plate or a shallow bowl that is small enough to fit inside the basket and sprinkle over some seasoning. Put the chicken breast on top and trickle over the marinade juices. Sprinkle over the five spice powder. Spoon over the sesame oil and arrange the spring onion strips on top of the chicken.

❹ Carefully place the plate or bowl inside the steamer. Cover and steam for 10 minutes or until the chicken breast feels firm when pressed. Carefully remove the plate or bowl from the steamer, making sure the steam does not burn your hand. Serve on a warmed plate.

(5½ POINTS VALUE) Cajun combo

Takes 30 minutes

| serves **1** | *POINTS* values per recipe **5.5** | calories per serving **400** |

This easy and delicious Cajun dish from the American Deep South draws inspiration from the flavours of Spain.

50 g (1¾ oz) long grain rice
low fat cooking spray
1 celery stick, sliced
3 spring onions, chopped
½ small green pepper, de-seeded and chopped
1 small garlic clove, crushed
½ teaspoon Cajun seasoning, or according to taste
½ teaspoon fresh thyme leaves or ¼ teaspoon dried thyme
15 g (½ oz) chorizo sausage, sliced
1 tomato, chopped
50 g (1¾ oz) skinless, boneless cooked chicken, chopped
50 g (1¾ oz) large peeled prawns, defrosted if frozen
salt and freshly ground black pepper
sprigs of fresh thyme, to garnish

❶ Cook the rice in plenty of boiling, lightly salted water for about 12 minutes until tender.

❷ Meanwhile, heat a large frying pan or wok and lightly spray it with low fat cooking spray. Add the celery, spring onions, green pepper and garlic. Sauté them for about 3 minutes, until softened.

❸ Add the Cajun seasoning, thyme, chorizo sausage, tomato and chicken. Cook gently, stirring occasionally, for a further 5 minutes.

❹ Drain the rice thoroughly and then add it to the frying pan, stirring well to combine everything. Add the prawns and cook for another 2–3 minutes, until they are heated through. Season with salt and pepper and then serve, garnished with sprigs of thyme.

TOP TIP If you can't find Cajun seasoning, use 1 teaspoon of mild chilli powder and a pinch of cayenne pepper, adding more or less according to taste.

VARIATION Omit the sausage and chicken for a meatless version, and add another 50 g (1¾ oz) prawns. The *POINTS* values per serving will be 4.

 **Pizza marinara**

Takes 30 minutes + 1 hour rising

serves **2**   *POINTS* values per recipe **14.5**   calories per serving **518**

This seafood topped pizza goes perfectly with a 0 *POINTS* value mixed leaf salad with a lemony dressing.

FOR THE PIZZA DOUGH
150 g (5½ oz) plain flour, plus 1 tablespoon for kneading
1 teaspoon fast action yeast
½ teaspoon sugar
1 teaspoon olive oil
salt

FOR THE TOPPING
230 g can of chopped tomatoes
1 garlic clove, crushed
100 g (3½ oz) asparagus tips
½ red pepper, sliced thinly
125 g (4½ oz) prawns, defrosted if necessary
50 g (1¾ oz) light mozzarella cheese, diced

❶ Sift the flour into a mixing bowl, then stir in the yeast, sugar and ½ teaspoon salt. Make a well in the centre, pour in the oil and about 125 ml (4 fl oz) warm water – enough to bring the dough together. Turn out on to a floured surface and knead for 3 minutes until smooth. Return to the bowl, cover with clingfilm and leave to rise for 1 hour, or until doubled in bulk.

❷ Preheat the oven to Gas Mark 6/200°C/fan oven 180°C.

❸ Roll the pizza dough out to a 25 cm (10 inches) disc. Transfer to a baking sheet and form a slight lip around the edge of the base to hold in the filling.

❹ Tip the tomatoes into a small saucepan and add the garlic. Simmer for 5 minutes until slightly thickened. Meanwhile, cook the asparagus tips in boiling salted water for 3 minutes then drain well. Spread the tomato sauce over the pizza base, leaving a 2.5 cm (1 inch) border. Scatter the asparagus tips, red pepper, prawns and mozzarella over the pizza.

❺ Bake for 10–12 minutes and serve straight away.

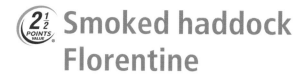

Smoked haddock Florentine

Takes 25 minutes

serves 2	*POINTS* values per recipe 5	calories per serving 225

A healthy alternative to the classic haddock and spinach combination.

2 x 150 g (5½ oz) undyed smoked haddock fillets, skinned
1 shallot or ½ small onion, chopped
250 g (9 oz) fresh baby spinach
1 tomato, de-seeded and diced
4 tablespoons half fat crème fraîche
2 tablespoons chopped fresh chives
salt and freshly ground black pepper

❶ Bring a frying pan, half filled with water, almost to the boil, then add the smoked haddock with the shallot or onion and poach gently for 4–5 minutes.

❷ Meanwhile, rinse the spinach and remove any tough stalks, then put it into a saucepan, with the water still clinging to the leaves. Cover and cook for 3–4 minutes until it is wilted. Drain well in a colander. Season to taste.

❸ Arrange the spinach between two hot plates and place a drained fish portion on top. Scatter the chopped tomato over each serving. Keep warm under the grill, on a low setting.

❹ Spoon 6 tablespoons of the fish liquor into a small pan. Boil rapidly, to reduce to 2 tablespoons, add the crème fraîche and the chives. Season with pepper. Spoon over the haddock and serve.

TOP TIP 1 Naturally smoked haddock develops an even yellow hue whereas when artificial dyes are applied they only give a vivid yellow colour on the surface of the fish.

TOP TIP 2 Very fresh smoked fish can be frozen for a maximum of 3 months, but do check with your fishmonger that the fish hasn't previously been frozen.

VARIATION 1 If you have enough *POINTS* values, poach an egg to serve on top of the haddock. This will add 1½ *POINTS* values per serving.

VARIATION 2 Use salmon fillets instead of haddock, and basil instead of chives. The *POINTS* values per serving will be 5.

(6½ POINTS VALUE) Spicy beef tacos

Takes 35 minutes

| serves **2** | **POINTS** values per recipe **13.5** | calories per serving **410** |

A fun and filling Mexican dish – perfect for a midweek supper.

low fat cooking spray
1 onion, chopped
1 garlic clove, crushed
1 green pepper, de-seeded and chopped
1 red pepper, de-seeded and chopped
½ teaspoon cayenne pepper
200 g (7 oz) extra lean minced beef
1 tablespoon tomato purée
4 taco shells
50 g (1¾ oz) half fat Cheddar cheese, grated
salt and freshly ground black pepper
0 **POINTS** value crisp green salad, to serve

❶ Heat a frying pan and spray with low fat cooking spray. Add the onion, garlic and peppers and cook for 3–4 minutes, until starting to soften.

❷ Sprinkle in the cayenne pepper and add the minced beef. Cook for 4–5 minutes, stirring occasionally, to brown all the meat.

❸ Add the tomato purée, 100 ml (3½ fl oz) water and seasoning and bring to a simmer. Simmer for 12–15 minutes, until the liquid has been absorbed.

❹ Heat the taco shells according to the instructions on the pack.

❺ Spoon the spicy mince mixture into each taco shell. Sprinkle each one with grated cheese and serve with a crisp green 0 **POINTS** value salad.

TOP TIP Taco shells can normally be found in most large supermarkets – look near the spicy canned and packet foods.

VARIATION Minced lamb, turkey or chicken could also be used for this recipe. The **POINTS** values per serving will be 7½, 5½ and 5 respectively.

(3) Hot spiced chick peas

Takes 20 minutes

serves **2**	**POINTS** values per recipe **6**	calories per serving **205**	V

This spicy meal is delicious served with 1 medium slice of bread (1 **POINTS** value) and salad, or 4 tablespoons plain boiled rice (3 **POINTS** values). Remember to add the extra **POINTS** values per serving.

1 teaspoon olive oil
1 small onion, chopped
1 teaspoon turmeric
½ teaspoon cumin seeds
1 teaspoon garam masala
4 large firm tomatoes, chopped roughly
425 g can of chick peas, drained
2 teaspoons lemon juice
2 tablespoons chopped fresh coriander
salt and freshly ground black pepper
coriander leaves, to garnish

❶ Heat the oil in a small saucepan, add the onion and cook for 5–10 minutes, stirring constantly, until golden brown.

❷ Add the spices and cook for a further minute. Add the tomatoes, chick peas, lemon juice and coriander. Season well, to taste. Cook for 1–2 minutes.

❸ Spoon into a warmed bowl, garnish with coriander and serve immediately.

TOP TIP Buy spices in small quantities as both the colour and flavour deteriorate over time. Store them in a dark dry cupboard. Start with a good basic range and increase the selection as you begin to experiment with new flavours.

VARIATION For a light snack for four, divide the spicy chick peas between four baked potatoes, and garnish each with 1 tablespoon of low fat plain yogurt. This will be 4 **POINTS** values per serving.

(7½ POINTS VALUE) Broccoli and blue cheese pasta

Takes 20 minutes

| serves **2** | ***POINTS*** values per recipe **14.5** | calories per serving **455** | **V** |

Blue cheese has a full flavour so a little goes a long way. It's great for adding a superb taste to pasta without adding too many extra ***POINTS*** values.

100 g (3½ oz) pasta shapes
250 g (9 oz) broccoli
170 g can of sweetcorn, drained
300 ml (½ pint) skimmed milk
1 tablespoon cornflour
50 g (1¾ oz) firm blue cheese (e.g. Stilton)
a good pinch of dried mixed herbs
salt and freshly ground black pepper

❶ Cook the pasta in lightly salted, boiling water according to the pack instructions. Drain and rinse it in cold water, and then tip it into a big bowl.

❷ Chop the stalk of the broccoli and cut the florets into small pieces. In lightly salted, boiling water blanch the pieces of stalk for 3 minutes, and then add the florets and cook for another 2 minutes. Drain, then mix the broccoli and sweetcorn with the pasta.

❸ In a heatproof jug, blend a little milk with the cornflour to make a paste. Pour the rest of the milk in a saucepan and bring it to the boil. When it starts to bubble, pour it over the blended cornflour, whisking continuously. Return the mixture to the pan and stir it over a low heat until it thickens.

❹ Remove the pan from the heat and crumble the cheese into the sauce. Add the herbs and seasoning.

❺ Mix together the pasta mixture with the sauce, and heat gently until bubbling. Serve immediately.

TOP TIP If you love blue cheese, then look out for the traditional British cheese, Blue Vinney, which is naturally lower in **POINTS** values than others. It is now sold in most supermarkets.

VARIATION Substitute 100 g (3½ oz) halved baby new potatoes for the pasta. The ***POINTS*** values will be reduced to 5½ per serving.

 # Lamb cutlets with caramelised onions

Takes 25 minutes

serves **2**	*POINTS* values per recipe **11**	calories per serving **140**	

1 large red or white onion, sliced thinly
a pinch of dried rosemary
2 teaspoons mint jelly
4 lean lamb cutlets (75 g/2¾ oz each)
salt and freshly ground black pepper

❶ Put the onion and rosemary in a small saucepan with 100 ml (3½ fl oz) water. Bring to a rapid boil. Cover and simmer for 10 minutes.

❷ Preheat the grill.

❸ Stir the mint jelly into the onions. Simmer, uncovered, for 5 minutes, stirring occasionally. Season with salt and pepper.

❹ Grill the cutlets for 2–3 minutes on either side. Serve with the sticky minted onions.

VARIATION For honey, thyme and balsamic onions, replace the mint jelly with 1 teaspoon runny honey and a few drops of balsamic vinegar. Add 1 teaspoon fresh chopped thyme.

(2) POINTS VALUE Lemon glazed turkey with mange tout peas

Takes 15 minutes

| serves **2** | ***POINTS*** values per recipe **4.5** | calories per serving **180** | |

Serve sizzling, stuffed into pitta bread pockets with loads of crisp salad leaves, or with plain boiled rice, adding the ***POINTS*** values as necessary.

225 g (8 oz) turkey breast strips (look out for stir fry packs or escalopes)
125 g (4½ oz) mange tout peas, trimmed
2 spring onions, sliced
1 tablespoon clear honey
juice of ½ a lemon (2 tablespoons)
1 tablespoon chopped fresh basil leaves
1 teaspoon sesame seeds
salt and freshly ground black pepper

❶ Briskly dry fry the turkey in a non stick frying pan over a high heat for 3–4 minutes until the meat is well sealed and lightly coloured.

❷ Add the mange tout peas and spring onions with 1 or 2 tablespoons of water if needed and stir fry for a further 3–4 minutes. Add the honey, lemon juice, chopped basil and sesame seeds. Season well.

❸ Let the juices come to the boil, coating the turkey with the glaze that is forming. Serve immediately.

0 *POINTS* value stuffed peppers

Takes 10 minutes to prepare, 15 minutes to cook

| serves **2** | *POINTS* values per recipe **0** | calories per serving **70** | **V** |

For a wonderful, tasty treat, it's hard to beat these halved peppers filled with colourful vegetables. Serve them warm for a 0 *POINTS* value starter.

1 red pepper
1 yellow pepper
1 courgette, sliced thinly
low fat cooking spray
8 cherry tomatoes, halved
2 good pinches of dried oregano
salt and freshly ground black pepper

❶ Halve the peppers lengthways and remove the seeds and membranes. Trim the stalks but do not pull them off.

❷ Heat the oven to Gas Mark 7/220°C/fan oven 200°C. Bring a large saucepan of water to the boil, add the courgette slices and blanch them for 1 minute. Drain them well and spray them with low fat cooking spray, carefully tossing them to coat the slices. Season to taste.

❸ Place the courgette slices in the pepper halves. Lay the tomatoes on top of the courgettes, cut side up. Season again and sprinkle over the herbs.

❹ Bake for 15 minutes, until the peppers and tomatoes start to soften. Allow them to cool slightly before serving.

Leek and mushroom gratin

Takes 25 minutes

| serves **2** | **POINTS** values per recipe **4.5** | calories per serving **100** | **V** |

A fantastic starter that tastes wonderfully indulgent, without using too many **POINTS** values.

low fat cooking spray
1 large leek, sliced thinly
125 g (4½ oz) mushrooms, sliced thinly
1 large garlic clove, chopped
1 tablespoon light soy sauce
2 tablespoons single cream
1 tablespoon chopped fresh parsley
1 tablespoon Parmesan cheese, grated
1 tablespoon dried natural coloured breadcrumbs
salt and freshly ground black pepper

❶ Heat a large saucepan and spray it with low fat cooking spray. Add the leek, mushrooms and garlic with 4 tablespoons of water and cook until the mixture sizzles. Cover and cook on a medium heat for 10 minutes, shaking the pan occasionally, until the vegetables have softened.

❷ Add the soy sauce and seasoning, and then mix in the cream and the parsley.

❸ Preheat the grill. Divide the leek and mushroom mixture between two ramekin dishes. Mix together the Parmesan cheese and breadcrumbs and then scatter this over the leek and mushrooms.

❹ Place the dishes under the preheated grill, until the tops are crisp and golden brown. Cool slightly and serve.

Greek pasta

Takes 15 minutes

| serves **2** | **POINTS** values per recipe **10.5** | calories per serving **325** | **V** |

Pasta is so versatile and this unusual dish is simply delicious.

120 g (4 oz) pasta
garlic low fat cooking spray
100 g (3½ oz) courgettes, halved and sliced
100 g (3½ oz) tomatoes, skins and seeds removed, flesh diced
50 g (1¾ oz) feta cheese, crumbled
10 olives, sliced or halved

❶ Cook the pasta in boiling water until just tender.

❷ Meanwhile, using a non stick frying pan and the low fat cooking spray, quickly brown the courgettes.

❸ When the pasta is cooked, drain and mix with all the other ingredients. Serve immediately.

Glazed sausage kebabs

Takes 10 minutes to prepare, 15 minutes to cook

makes **8**   *POINTS* values per recipe **11**   calories per kebab **135**

450 g (1 lb) 99% fat free sausages, each cut into three
2 courgettes, sliced thickly
8 small tomatoes, halved
2 dessert apples, cored, quartered and cut into eighths
4 small onions, quartered

FOR THE GLAZE
2 tablespoons mango chutney
2 tablespoons orange juice
1 tablespoon coarse grain mustard
½ teaspoon ground ginger

❶ To make the glaze, gently heat all the ingredients together in a small pan.

❷ Heat the grill to medium. Thread the sausages, courgettes, tomatoes, apples and onions alternately on to eight small metal skewers.

❸ Grill the kebabs for 12–15 minutes, turning and brushing them with the glaze. Mix any pan juices with any left over marinade and dribble this over the kebabs.

TOP TIP Soak wooden skewers in water first to prevent them from catching fire.

VARIATION Replace the apples with chunks of pineapple or apricot halves and use the natural juice from the cans instead of the orange juice in the glaze. Adjust the *POINTS* values if necessary.

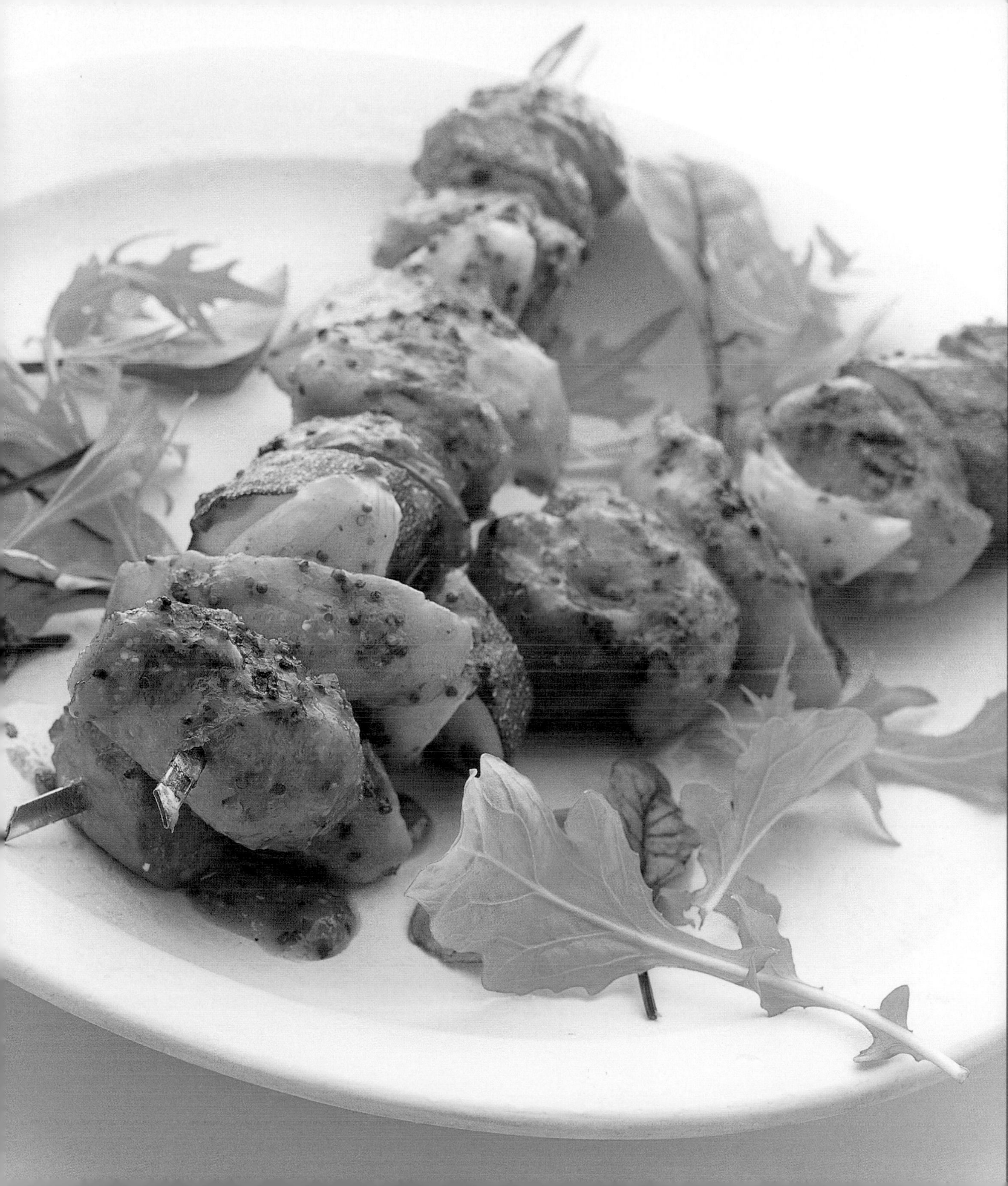

Quick and slow recipes

(2½) Garlic prawns

Takes 10 minutes

serves **4**   **POINTS** values per recipe **9.5**   calories per serving **180**

low fat cooking spray
3 garlic cloves, sliced thinly
1 red chilli, de-seeded and chopped finely (optional)
400 g (14 oz) large, frozen, cooked and peeled prawns
a small bunch of parsley, chopped
juice of 1 lemon
salt
4 medium slices of crusty bread, to serve

❶ Spray a large frying pan with the cooking spray, then add the garlic and chilli, if using. Stir fry for 2 minutes. Add the prawns and 4 tablespoons of water. Sprinkle with a little salt.

❷ Stir fry for another 3 or 4 minutes, then add the chopped parsley. Squeeze over the lemon juice and then spoon on to serving plates. Serve with the bread to mop up the juices.

(3) Cullen skink

Takes 15 minutes to prepare, 15 minutes to cook

serves **4**   **POINTS** values per recipe **13**   calories per serving **235**

This traditional Scottish soup is named after a small fishing port in Scotland.

400 g (14 oz) smoked haddock fillets
1 bay leaf
400 ml (14 fl oz) semi skimmed milk
1 teaspoon unsalted butter
1 large onion, chopped
3 x 150 g (5½ oz) potatoes, peeled and diced
salt and freshly ground black pepper
freshly chopped chives or parsley, to serve

❶ Place the haddock fillets and bay leaf in a medium saucepan and cover with the milk. Simmer for 6–8 minutes, and then drain and reserve the milk and fish. Flake the fish into bite size pieces.

❷ Melt the butter in a medium saucepan and sauté the onion for 3–4 minutes.

❸ Add the potatoes and stir before adding the reserved milk.

❹ Simmer for 15–18 minutes.

❺ Add the fish and cook for a further 2–3 minutes. Check the seasoning and serve in four warmed bowls sprinkled with freshly chopped chives or parsley.

TOP TIP Dyed smoked haddock tastes no different, but looks so much better in this recipe.

VARIATION You can use smoked cod in this dish if you can't find smoked haddock. The **POINTS** values per serving will be 3½.

(6½) Tuna pasta bake

Takes 25 minutes

serves **4**   *POINTS* values per recipe **26.5**   calories per serving **420**   ❄

A great family favourite from America, this quick budget dish is bound to please everyone, and the all in one sauce is so easy to make – fantastic!

250 g (9 oz) pasta shapes
1 onion, chopped
400 ml (14 fl oz) skimmed milk
2 tablespoons cornflour
100 g (3½ oz) frozen peas, defrosted
200 g can of tuna in brine, drained and flaked
50 g (1½ oz) half fat Cheddar cheese, grated
15 g (½ oz) Parmesan cheese, grated
2 tablespoons natural colour dried breadcrumbs
6–8 cherry tomatoes, halved
salt and freshly ground black pepper

❶ Cook the pasta with the onion in a large saucepan of lightly salted, boiling water according to the pack instructions. Drain and rinse in cold water. Set it aside.

❷ While the pasta is cooking, make the sauce. In a heatproof jug, mix 3 tablespoons of the milk with the cornflour to make a smooth paste. In a large saucepan, put the rest of the milk on to boil and when the liquid starts to creep up the sides of the pan, pour it over the cornflour paste, whisking as you do so.

❸ Return the milk mixture to the pan and cook, stirring, on a low heat until it thickens. Add the peas and tuna, and then simmer for 2 minutes. Remove the pan from the heat and cool slightly.

❹ Mix in all the Cheddar cheese and half of the Parmesan cheese. Stir the cooked pasta into the sauce. Check the seasoning. Reheat it all gently in the pan but do not allow it to boil.

❺ Preheat the grill. Transfer the pasta mixture into an ovenproof dish. Mix the remaining Parmesan cheese with the breadcrumbs and scatter this over the top. Arrange the tomato halves, cut side up, over the breadcrumb topping.

❻ Place the dish under the grill and cook until the top is crispy and golden. Serve on four warmed plates.

Quick prawn and crab noodles

Takes 25 minutes

serves **4**   *POINTS* values per recipe **19.5**   calories per serving **440**

Frozen prawns and crab sticks make a quick meal when combined with instant egg noodles and a few vegetables.

1 tablespoon tomato purée
1 tablespoon light soy sauce
1 tablespoon cider or light malt vinegar
1 tablespoon dark or light muscovado sugar
2 teaspoons cornflour
225 g (8 oz) thread egg noodles
2 teaspoons stir fry oil or vegetable oil
1 red pepper, de-seeded and sliced finely
1 bunch of spring onions, trimmed and sliced finely
1 courgette, sliced
100 g (3½ oz) mange tout peas, sliced
225 g (8 oz) large peeled prawns, defrosted if frozen
8 frozen crab sticks, chopped into chunks
salt and freshly ground black pepper

❶ In a small bowl, mix together the tomato purée, soy sauce, vinegar, sugar and cornflour. Set aside.

❷ Soak the noodles in boiling water for about 6 minutes, or according to the pack instructions.

❸ Meanwhile, heat the oil in a wok or large frying pan. Add the pepper, spring onions, courgette and mange tout peas and stir fry over a high heat for about 3–4 minutes.

❹ Add the prawns and crab sticks and cook, stirring, for about 2 minutes until hot. Stir the soy sauce mixture, add to the wok or frying pan and cook, stirring constantly, until thickened and blended. Season to taste.

❺ Drain the noodles and divide between four warmed serving plates. Pile the prawn mixture on top, then serve at once.

TOP TIP Muscovado sugar gives a lovely flavour to the sweet and sour sauce in this recipe; it doesn't really matter whether you use the light or dark variety. If you haven't got any to hand, you could use ordinary brown sugar although the flavour will not be quite as nice.

1½ Spinach and cheese rolls

Takes 10 minutes to prepare, 15 minutes to bake

serves 4 | ***POINTS*** values per recipe **6.5** | calories per serving **135** | **V**

Creamy spinach rolled into light and crispy filo pastry makes a tasty and attractive meal. Serve these rolls warm with a 0 ***POINTS*** value green salad and sliced tomato.

250 g pack of baby spinach leaves
200 g tub of reduced fat cottage cheese, ideally with chives
1 tablespoon chopped fresh dill or 1 teaspoon dried dill
4 x 30 cm x 17 cm (12 inch x 6½ inch) sheets of filo pastry
1 tablespoon low fat spread, melted
salt and freshly ground black pepper

❶ Cook the spinach according to the pack instructions, either in the microwave or in a large saucepan. Drain it well, pressing out as much water as possible.

❷ Chop the spinach finely, and then mix it with the cottage cheese, dill and seasoning.

❸ Preheat the oven to Gas Mark 6/200°C/fan oven 180°C. Using a pastry brush, dab the filo sheets with the melted low fat spread. Divide the spinach filling into four and place along the bottom of each sheet, spreading it out to flatten it slightly. Roll each sheet up firmly, but not too tightly.

❹ Place the rolls on a non stick baking sheet. Bake them for 15 minutes until they are crisp and golden. Slice them in half on the diagonal and serve them warm.

VARIATION This spinach and cottage cheese filling works brilliantly in jacket potatoes, but remember to alter the ***POINTS*** values accordingly.

4½ Feta stuffed pitta

POINTS VALUE

Takes 5 minutes

serves **1**   *POINTS* values per recipe **4.5**   calories per serving **230**   V

To vary this recipe, you can also add a little chopped garlic or mint sauce to the stuffing.

1 medium wholemeal pitta bread, warmed and halved

FOR THE STUFFING
25 g (1 oz) feta cheese, crumbled
a few slices of red onion or spring onion
2 cherry tomatoes, or 1 standard tomato, halved or cut into wedges
a few slices of crispy lettuce (Iceberg or Little Gem)
1 teaspoon lemon juice
black pepper

❶ Mix all the stuffing ingredients together, then use to stuff the pitta bread.

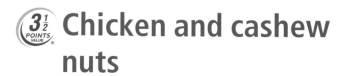 # Chicken and cashew nuts

Takes 30 minutes

serves **4**   *POINTS* values per recipe **13.5**   calories per serving **260**

Toasted cashew nuts give this colourful stir fry an extra crunch. As with all stir fried dishes, make sure everything is prepared before you actually start to cook, as the pace is fast and furious! Serve with 4 tablespoons of cooked rice, adding an extra 3 *POINTS* values per serving.

1 teaspoon sunflower oil
40 g (1½ oz) cashew nuts, halved
350 g (12 oz) skinless, boneless chicken breast, diced
2 teaspoons sesame oil
2 carrots, peeled and cut into thin batons
150 g (5½ oz) baby corn, cut into thirds
100 g (3½ oz) mange tout, halved
2 garlic cloves, sliced
1 bunch of spring onions, cut into 2.5 cm (1 inch) lengths, reserving some, sliced finely, to garnish
2 tablespoons soy sauce
1 tablespoon dry sherry
½ pint (300 ml) chicken stock
1 tablespoon cornflour

❶ Heat the sunflower oil in a wok or a large non stick frying pan and gently brown the cashew nuts. Remove with a draining spoon and keep to one side.

❷ Coat the chicken in the sesame oil then tip into the hot wok and cook for 3 minutes, stirring occasionally, until browned.

❸ Add the carrots, baby corn, mange tout and garlic and stir fry for 2 minutes.

❹ Stir in the spring onions, soy sauce and sherry and cook for 1 minute.

❺ Return the cashew nuts to the wok, add the chicken stock, cover and simmer for 5 minutes.

❻ Blend the cornflour with 1 tablespoon of cold water, then stir into the sauce until slightly thickened. Serve immediately.

VARIATION For a vegetarian version, swap the chicken breast with the same weight of Quorn pieces, and use vegetable stock instead of chicken. The *POINTS* values will then be 3 per serving.

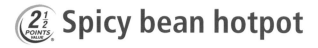 **Spicy bean hotpot**

Takes 15 minutes to prepare, 20–30 minutes to cook

| serves **4** | *POINTS* values per recipe **10.5** | calories per serving **175** | ❄ | **V** |

low fat cooking spray

1 red onion, chopped

2 carrots, peeled and chopped

2 celery sticks, chopped

1 red pepper, de-seeded and chopped

1 teaspoon ground cumin

1 teaspoon curry powder

½ teaspoon ground ginger

415 g (14½ oz) canned Weight Watchers from Heinz Baked Beans

420 g (14¾ oz) canned red kidney beans, rinsed and drained

salt and freshly ground black pepper

a bunch of fresh parsley, chopped, to garnish

❶ Heat a medium saucepan and spray with low fat cooking spray. Add the onion, carrots, celery and red pepper and cook for 4–5 minutes, stirring occasionally.

❷ Add the spices and mix well. Cook for another 1–2 minutes.

❸ Pour in the baked beans and kidney beans and 200 ml (7 fl oz) of water. Bring to the boil and then simmer, covered, for 15 minutes.

❹ Check the seasoning and sprinkle in the parsley before serving in big bowls.

VARIATION For those that miss their meat, you can add bacon or low fat sausages to this dish. Chop 100 g (3½ oz) bacon or low fat sausages and add with the vegetables at the beginning. The *POINTS* values per serving if using bacon will be 4 and if using sausages 3½.

Red and green pepper burritos

4 POINTS VALUE

Takes 15 minutes to prepare, 15 minutes to cook

| serves **4** | *POINTS* values per recipe **15** | calories per serving **255** | **V** |

A delicious vegetarian version of this popular Mexican dish. Serve with a crunchy 0 *POINTS* value green salad.

low fat cooking spray
1 large onion, sliced
½ teaspoon chilli powder
1 red pepper, de-seeded and sliced
1 green pepper, de-seeded and sliced
100 g (3½ oz) canned red kidney beans, drained
4 soft flour tortillas
100 g (3½ oz) low fat plain yogurt
75 g (2¾ oz) half fat Cheddar cheese, grated

❶ Heat the low fat cooking spray in a large frying pan. Add the onion and sauté for 2–3 minutes on a gentle heat.

❷ Add the chilli powder and stir well before adding the red and green peppers. Cook for another 8–10 minutes, stirring occasionally until the peppers have softened and the onion is starting to caramelise slightly.

❸ Add the kidney beans and cook for 3–4 minutes.

❹ Preheat the grill.

❺ Heat the flour tortillas according to the pack instructions.

❻ Divide the low fat yogurt between the four tortillas, spreading it over the centre of each one. Divide the pepper mixture between the tortillas and wrap or fold each one and place in a shallow heatproof dish.

❼ Sprinkle the burritos with the grated cheese and place under the grill until the cheese is bubbling and melted.

Gammon and spiced pineapple

6½ POINTS VALUE

Takes 10 minutes

| serves **2** | *POINTS* values per recipe **12.5** | calories per serving **316** |

A slightly spicy, sweet and sour sauce lends a twist to this old favourite. Serve with some broccoli and 100 g (3½ oz) boiled new potatoes for an extra 1 *POINTS* value per serving.

2 x 150 g (5½ oz) gammon plate steaks
220 g can of sliced pineapples in juice
¼ teaspoon ground mixed spice
1 tablespoon cider vinegar or white wine vinegar
1 teaspoon cornflour
low fat cooking spray

❶ Cook the gammon steaks for 8–10 minutes under a preheated grill, turning half way through cooking.

❷ Meanwhile, drain the juice from the pineapple into a jug and whisk in the mixed spice, vinegar and 3 tablespoons of water. In a small bowl, blend the cornflour with 1 tablespoon of water.

❸ Heat a non stick frying pan on the hob. Pat the pineapple rings dry on kitchen paper, spray the pan with low fat cooking spray then fry the pineapple rings for 2 minutes on each side until caramelised.

❹ Pour the pineapple juice mixture into the frying pan and bubble for 30 seconds until slightly reduced. Add the blended cornflour and stir until thickened.

❺ Serve the gammon steaks on warmed plates, topped with the caramelised pineapple and sauce.

quick & slow recipes 67

(4) Three minute trifle

Takes 3 minutes

serves **4**	*POINTS* values per recipe **16**	calories per serving **120**	**V**

A very simple dessert that's always a favourite. Use any combination of canned fruit as long as they are in natural juice.

4 sponge fingers
225 g (8 oz) canned mandarins in natural juice
400 g (14 oz) canned low fat custard
low fat aerosol cream

❶ Break each sponge finger into small pieces and arrange in the base of four individual glass serving dishes.

❷ Divide the mandarins equally over each dish with 1 tablespoon of the juice.

❸ Top each with custard and finally, just as you serve, a swirl of cream (about 1 tablespoon for each trifle).

(4) Quick fruit crumble

Takes 10 minutes to prepare, 20 minutes to cook

serves **4**	*POINTS* values per recipe **15.5**	calories per serving **240**	❄	**V**

This simple and satisfying dessert is assembled in no time using a can of fruit and a quickly whizzed up crumble topping – just right for a mid week pudding. Serve this with low fat natural yogurt or low fat custard, adding the extra *POINTS* values.

420 g can of peaches in natural juice, drained
1 large ripe banana, sliced thinly
50 g (1¾ oz) low fat spread
100 g (3½ oz) plain white flour
1 tablespoon light soft brown sugar
2 tablespoons porridge oats
freshly grated nutmeg

❶ Preheat the oven to Gas Mark 5/190°C/fan oven 170°C.

❷ Tip the canned fruit into a medium size baking dish – chop the fruit if necessary. Mix in the banana slices.

❸ Place the low fat spread, flour and sugar in a food processor and whiz until the mixture resembles fine breadcrumbs. Stir in the porridge oats. Spoon this topping over the fruit and sprinkle nutmeg over.

❹ Place the dish on a baking tray and bake in the oven for 20 minutes until the topping is lightly browned.

VARIATION In spring, try 400 g (14 oz) tender, pink forced rhubarb instead of the peaches. There's no need to pre-cook it. Chop it and add 1 tablespoon caster sugar. The *POINTS* values are 3½ per serving.

② ½ Almond meringue peaches

Preparation time 3 minutes, grilling time 5 minutes

serves **4**	*POINTS* values per recipe **9**	calories per serving **305**		**V**

8 fresh peach halves (stones removed)
8 amaretti biscuits
2 tablespoons Amaretto or Cointreau liqueur
1 egg white
30 g (1¼ oz) caster sugar
15 g (½ oz) flaked almonds

❶ Preheat the grill to low or medium. Place the peach halves, hollow side up, in a tart or Yorkshire pudding baking tin that will fit in your grill pan (the holes in the tin will help keep the peaches upright).

❷ Place a biscuit in each peach hollow and drizzle a little of the liqueur over each.

❸ In a large, clean bowl whisk the egg white until stiff, then gradually whisk in the caster sugar. Put a spoonful of meringue over each peach.

❹ Place under the grill and cook slowly for 3–4 minutes. Watch to make sure they don't start to brown too quickly. Sprinkle the almonds over the top and continue to grill until the meringue and nuts have turned golden. Transfer the peaches to four small plates and serve immediately.

(4½ POINTS VALUE) Roast ham with spicy plum glaze

Takes 10 minutes to prepare, 3 hours to cook

serves **8**   *POINTS* values per recipe **36.5**   calories per serving **350**   ❄

Leftover ham can be used for tasty sandwich fillings, or tossed into a mid week pasta bake. A great Christmas centrepiece too!

2.25 kg (5 lb) unsmoked gammon joint

FOR THE GLAZE
125 g (4½ oz) plum jam
2 tablespoons orange, lemon or apple juice
1 teaspoon ground ginger
2 teaspoons chilli sauce

❶ Preheat the oven to Gas Mark 5/190°C/fan oven 170°C.

❷ Wrap the gammon joint in foil and place in a roasting tin. Roast in the oven for 3 hours (65 minutes per kilo/30 minutes per lb, plus 30 minutes extra).

❸ To make the glaze, place all the ingredients in a small pan and gently heat together.

❹ Remove the foil for the last 30 minutes of cooking, brush half the glaze over the joint and return to the oven, uncovered. Repeat 10 minutes later.

❺ At the end of the cooking time, remove the ham to a serving platter, and brush any remaining glaze from the roasting pan over the top. Carve into thin slices, and serve 175 g (6 oz) ham per person.

TOP TIP For a cold eating joint, cook the ham up to three days in advance, wrap in foil and refrigerate until required. It is also much easier to carve when completely cold.

VARIATION For an alternative glaze, replace the plum jam with orange marmalade, omit the chilli sauce and add a teaspoon of allspice or ground cinnamon with the ginger.

Irish beef stew with dumplings

6½ POINTS VALUE

Takes 25 minutes to prepare, 2 hours to cook

serves **4** *POINTS* values per recipe **25.5** calories per serving **405** ❄

To think that beef stew with dumplings was once regarded an economical, filling meal for all the family! Now you will find versions in top restaurants and food magazines – how trends have changed. Serve with 0 *POINTS* value carrots and cabbage for a great traditional meal.

1 tablespoon vegetable oil
500 g (1 lb 2 oz) lean braising steak, cubed
2 onions, cut into chunks
2 celery sticks, chopped
1 tablespoon plain flour
300 ml (½ pint) strong dark ale
300 ml (½ pint) beef stock
1 bay leaf
a few sprigs fresh thyme or 1 teaspoon dried thyme
250 g (9 oz) open mushrooms, halved
salt and freshly ground black pepper

FOR THE DUMPLINGS
100 g (3½ oz) plain flour
a pinch of salt
2 teaspoons dried mustard powder
40 g (1½ oz) low fat spread (e.g. St Ivel 'Gold')
1 tablespoon finely chopped fresh chives

❶ Preheat the oven to Gas Mark 3/160°C/fan oven 140°C. Heat the oil in a flameproof casserole dish and brown the meat all over. Remove with a slotted spoon. Add the onions and celery and cook for 5 minutes, stirring occasionally.

❷ Sprinkle in the flour, and gradually blend in the beer and stock. Add the bay leaf and thyme. Season with salt and pepper. Cover and transfer to the oven to cook for 1½ hours.

❸ Meanwhile, make the dumplings. Sift the flour, salt and mustard into a bowl. Rub in the low fat spread until the mixture resembles fine breadcrumbs. Stir in the chives and add just enough cold water to make a soft dough. Shape into eight small dumplings. Chill until required.

❹ After 1½ hours, remove the lid from the casserole, stir in the mushrooms and adjust the seasoning, to taste. Increase the oven temperature to Gas Mark 6/200°C/fan oven 180°C. Arrange the dumplings over the surface of the casserole and transfer to the highest shelf of the oven, without the lid and cook for a further 30 minutes until the dumplings are golden brown and crusty.

TOP TIP If you have a slow cooker, this recipe lends itself to long gentle cooking, so adapt the recipe according to the manufacturer's instructions.

VARIATION Vary the dumplings by replacing the mustard and chives with the same quantity of horseradish and parsley.

 **French lamb casserole**

Takes 10 minutes to prepare, 2½ hours to cook

serves **4**   *POINTS* values per recipe **25.5**   calories per serving **285**   ✳

This French dish cooks conveniently slowly in the oven while you go and do something else.

400 g (14 oz) dried haricot beans, soaked overnight
   or 2 x 300 g cans of haricot beans, drained
low fat cooking spray
2 onions, chopped
3 garlic cloves, crushed
250 g (9 oz) lean cubed lamb
2 tablespoons tomato purée
400 g can of chopped tomatoes
2 sprigs of thyme
2 sprigs of majoram
2 sprigs of parsley
1 celery stalk, chopped roughly
1 bay leaf
a handful of chopped fresh parsley, to garnish
salt and freshly ground black pepper

❶ If using the dried beans, drain the soaked beans and put in a saucepan. Cover with cold water. Bring to the boil and boil for 10 minutes, skimming occasionally. If using the canned beans, go directly to step 2.

❷ Preheat the oven to Gas Mark 4/180°C/fan oven 160°C. Spray a flameproof casserole with the cooking spray, then sauté the onions and garlic for 4 minutes on the hob. Add a couple of tablespoons of water if they stick. Add the meat and seal all over for 2 minutes.

❸ Add the rest of the ingredients and 450 ml (16 fl oz) of water. Cover and bake for 2 hours, stirring every now and then. Add the seasoning and serve sprinkled with some fresh parsley.

 Lasagne verde

Takes 20 minutes to prepare, 50 minutes to cook

serves **4**   *POINTS* values per recipe **27.5**   calories per serving **580**   ❄   **V**

A lovely twist on the traditional lasagne recipe.

250 g (9 oz) no pre cook lasagne sheets, preferably spinach

FOR THE FILLING
1 medium round lettuce, shredded
450 g (1 lb) frozen peas
125 ml (4 fl oz) vegetable stock
low fat cooking spray
2 garlic cloves, chopped finely
225 g (8 oz) courgettes, diced finely
125 ml (4 fl oz) white wine
a small bunch of fresh mint, chopped
500 g (1 lb 2 oz) frozen spinach, cooked
200 g (7 oz) Quark cheese
a pinch of freshly grated nutmeg
salt and freshly ground black pepper

FOR THE TOPPING
2 eggs
4 tablespoons skimmed milk
300 g (10½ oz) low fat plain yogurt
100 g (3½ oz) low fat soft cheese
50 g (1¾ oz) reduced fat, strong flavoured Cheddar cheese, grated

❶ Cook the lettuce with the peas and the stock in a covered saucepan for 20 minutes over a low heat.

❷ Meanwhile, heat a large frying pan. Spray with the cooking spray. Sauté the garlic for 2 minutes. Add the courgettes. Stir fry for 4 minutes over a high heat until the courgettes brown slightly. Add the wine. Boil rapidly until all but a few tablespoons evaporate. Add the mint, toss and remove from the heat.

❸ In another pan, gently heat the spinach and Quark. Add the nutmeg and seasoning.

❹ Preheat the oven to Gas Mark 6/200°C/fan oven 180°C. Spray a 30 cm (12 inch) ovenproof dish with the cooking spray then line the bottom with lasagne. Mix the cooked lettuce and peas together with the courgette mixture.

❺ Cover the bottom of the dish with a layer of vegetables in their juices, then top with lasagne and repeat twice more. Finish with a layer of lasagne.

❻ Beat together the topping ingredients, except the Cheddar cheese. Pour over the lasagne. Sprinkle with cheese and bake for 30 minutes until golden.

(6) Home made pizza

Takes 20 minutes + 1 hour 10 minutes to 1 hour 40 minutes standing

serves **4**　**POINTS** values per recipe **24.5**　calories per serving **355**　**V**

Making your own pizza is such good fun, especially if you have children to help you. Pizza taste great and the best part is that it is so low in **POINTS** values.

FOR THE BASE
200 g (7 oz) strong white flour plus 2 teaspoons for rolling
½ teaspoon salt
½ sachet dried yeast
low fat cooking spray

FOR THE TOPPING
400 g (14 oz) canned chopped tomatoes
300 g (10½ oz) frozen spinach, defrosted and drained
2 tomatoes, sliced
2 spring onions, chopped
70 g (2½ oz) grated mozzarella light cheese
150 g (5½ oz) grated half fat Cheddar
salt and freshly ground black pepper

① Place the flour and salt in a large bowl. Make a well in the centre and add 125 ml (4½ fl oz) tepid water.

② Sprinkle over the yeast and leave to stand for 5 minutes.

③ Stir the water to dissolve the yeast and gradually draw in the flour to make a soft dough.

④ Turn out the dough on to a floured surface and knead the dough until smooth.

⑤ Spray a clean bowl with low fat cooking spray. Cover and leave it to rise until doubled in size. This will take about 1–1½ hours.

⑥ Punch the dough to take out the air.

⑦ Shape the dough into a ball. Cover it with a cloth and leave to rest for 10 minutes.

⑧ Place the dough ball on a lightly floured surface and roll to a 30 cm (12 inch) round. Place the dough on a baking sheet.

⑨ Preheat the oven to its hottest temperature and place the shelves near the top.

⑩ Spread the tomatoes over the dough, then top with the remaining ingredients, finishing with the cheeses. Spread the toppings evenly, leaving a small clean edge around the dough. Bake in the oven for 8–10 minutes, until the base of the pizza is golden.

TOP TIP Try not to add too much flour when kneading and rolling, as this will make the dough tougher and not so light.

VARIATION For a different topping, use 400 g (14 oz) canned chopped tomatoes, 1 sliced courgette, 1 de-seeded and sliced red pepper, 90 g (3¼ oz) watercress, 100 g (3½ oz) drained, canned tuna in brine. Season to taste. The **POINTS** values per pizza will be 5½ without cheese.

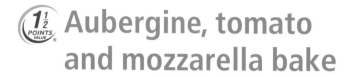

Aubergine, tomato and mozzarella bake

Takes 15 minutes to prepare, 1½ hours to cook

| serves **6** | *POINTS* values per recipe **10** | calories per serving **160** | **V** |

Enjoy a touch of Italian sunshine on a winter evening; this is an ideal supper to enjoy with friends – or on a tray in front of the TV. Serve with a crisp green salad to keep the *POINTS* values low.

2 x 400 g cans of chopped tomatoes
2 garlic cloves, crushed
2 tablespoons chopped fresh basil (or 1 teaspoon dried)
1 teaspoon grated lemon rind
a pinch of sugar
4 large red peppers, de-seeded and quartered
1 tablespoon olive oil
3 aubergines, sliced into 2 cm (¾ inch) rounds
125 g (4½ oz) mozzarella 'light' cheese, drained and sliced thinly
50 g (2 oz) freshly grated Parmesan cheese
salt and freshly ground black pepper

❶ Place the tomatoes in a saucepan with the garlic, basil, lemon rind and sugar. Season well. Cover and simmer for 30 minutes then remove the lid and simmer for a further 15 minutes. Cool.

❷ Preheat the oven to Gas Mark 6/200°C/fan oven 180°C.

❸ Place the peppers, skin side up, on a grill pan, brush lightly with oil and grill for 4–5 minutes until charred and blistered. Transfer to a bowl, cover with clingfilm and leave to cool. Brush the aubergine slices with the remaining oil and grill for 5–6 minutes on each side then remove from the heat and leave to cool. Peel the peppers.

❹ Spoon a little tomato sauce into the base of a large, shallow ovenproof dish and top with a layer of peppers and aubergine. Arrange half the mozzarella slices over then repeat, with more vegetables, finishing with the mozzarella. Sprinkle with Parmesan.

❺ Bake in the oven for 30–40 minutes, until bubbling and golden brown. Serve immediately.

Sticky toffee pudding

(5 POINTS VALUE)

Takes 10 minutes to prepare, 45 minutes to cook

serves **6** *POINTS* values per recipe **31** calories per serving **355** ❄ **V**

This good old fashioned British pudding can tempt even the strongest willed Weight Watchers Member! But there is no need to miss out on scrumptious treats, as this recipe proves.

low fat cooking spray
175 g (6 oz) stoned dates, chopped
1 teaspoon bicarbonate of soda
175 g (6 oz) self raising flour
175 g (6 oz) dark muscovado sugar
50 g (1¾ oz) low fat spread
3 tablespoons skimmed milk
1 teaspoon vanilla essence
2 egg whites, whisked to soft peaks

FOR THE STICKY SAUCE
1 tablespoon dark muscovado sugar
1 tablespoon golden syrup
4 tablespoons virtually fat free fromage frais

❶ Preheat the oven to Gas Mark 5/190°C/fan oven 170°C. Spray a 19 cm (7 inch) square cake tin with the low fat cooking spray and line the base with baking paper.

❷ Place the dates in a small pan with 200 ml (7 fl oz) of water. Bring to the boil, then simmer for 5 minutes by which time the dates will have absorbed most of the water. Stir in the bicarbonate of soda.

❸ Place the flour, sugar and low fat spread in a bowl and rub together until the fat has been incorporated into the flour and the mixture is crumbly. Stir in the milk, vanilla essence and dates then fold in the lightly beaten egg whites. Spoon the mixture into the cake tin and level the surface. Bake for 35 minutes or until well risen and firm.

❹ To make the sauce, place all the ingredients in a small pan and heat until melted and smooth. Do not allow the mixture to boil.

❺ Serve the pudding warm, with a drizzle of the sauce.

VARIATION This pudding is also delicious eaten cold, so save a slice for a day later, to enjoy with a cup of coffee. Serve the pudding as a tea time cake, if you wish. Dust the surface with sieved icing sugar and add no extra *POINTS* values.

(6) Baked lime cheesecake

Takes 15 minutes to prepare, 1 hour to cook + 2 hours cooling

serves **10**   *POINTS* values per recipe **59.5**   calories per serving **275**   **V**

A creamy, sharp topping and a crunchy ginger base make this the perfect cheesecake. Serve with fresh fruits if you have *POINTS* values to spare.

low fat cooking spray
180 g (6¼ oz) gingernut biscuits, crushed
40 g (1½ oz) low fat spread, melted
300 g (10½ oz) Quark
200 g (7 oz) cream cheese
60 g (2 oz) fruit sugar (fructose)
4 large eggs
finely grated zest and juice of 4 limes, plus extra to decorate

❶ Preheat the oven to Gas Mark 3/160°C/fan oven 140°C. Spray a 20 cm (8 inch) loose bottomed tin with low fat cooking spray.

❷ Mix the crushed biscuits and melted low fat spread together and press the mixture into the base of the tin.

❸ Bake in the oven for 10 minutes. Meanwhile, whisk together the Quark, cream cheese, fruit sugar and eggs until smooth.

❹ Beat in the grated lime zest and juice.

❺ Pour the cheese mixture over the baked biscuit base and return to the oven for 1 hour.

❻ After 1 hour, turn off the oven and leave the cheesecake for another 2 hours before removing and chilling in the fridge (the top may crack but that is fine). Decorate with the lime zest.

TOP TIP The quickest way to crush the gingernut biscuits is in a food processor, but don't over process them or you will have powder instead of nice chunky bits.

VARIATION Use lemons instead of limes if you wish. The *POINTS* values will remain the same.

3½ POINTS VALUE

Apricot and almond rice pudding crunch

Takes 10 minutes to prepare, 40–45 minutes to cook

serves **4**   *POINTS* values per recipe **14.5**   calories per serving **180**   **V**

A childhood favourite, rice pudding is simplicity itself to make and yet is still regarded as an indulgent treat.

FOR THE RICE PUDDING
50 g (1¾ oz) pudding rice
600 ml (1 pint) semi skimmed milk
25 g (1 oz) caster sugar
a few drops of vanilla essence
400 g can apricot halves in natural juice, drained

FOR THE TOPPING
grated rind of 1 orange
¼ teaspoon mixed spice
50 g (1¾ oz) demerara sugar
15 g (½ oz) chopped almonds

❶ Place the rice and milk in a pan and bring to the boil, stirring constantly. Simmer gently for 30–40 minutes or until tender, adding a little extra milk if necessary. Stir in the sugar and vanilla essence.

❷ Quarter the apricot halves and divide between the bases of four 125 ml (4 fl oz) ramekin dishes. Top with the rice pudding.

❸ Mix together the orange rind, spice, sugar and almonds and sprinkle evenly over the rice pudding.

❹ Transfer the ramekins to a baking sheet and place under a preheated hot grill for 5 minutes or until the sugar has caramelised and is bubbling and golden. Serve while still warm, or chill.

TOP TIP Use this recipe for rice pudding to serve with stewed fruits or a spoonful of sultanas or reduced sugar jam. On its own, the rice pudding is 2 *POINTS* values per serving.

VARIATION 1 Use 250 g (9 oz) fresh raspberries instead of the apricots and omit the orange rind from the topping. The *POINTS* values per serving will be the same.

VARIATION 2 For a special occasion, stir in 4 tablespoons of half fat crème fraîche. The *POINTS* values per serving will be 4.

(5½) Chicken curry

Takes 10 minutes to prepare, 55 minutes to cook

serves **4**	**POINTS** values per recipe **22.5**	calories per serving **400**	❄

This fruity chicken curry is absolutely delicious. Choose mild, medium or hot curry paste – depending on how hot and spicy you want it to be.

2 teaspoons vegetable oil

1 large onion, chopped

1 apple, chopped

2 garlic cloves, crushed

1 large carrot, sliced

1 parsnip, chopped

2 tablespoons curry paste (mild, medium or hot, according to taste)

450 g (1 lb) skinless, boneless chicken breasts, cut into chunks

450 ml (16 fl oz) chicken stock

25 g (1 oz) sultanas

1 tablespoon chopped fresh coriander or mint

150 g (5½ oz) basmati or long grain rice

1 banana

salt and freshly ground black pepper

TO SERVE

4 tablespoons plain low fat yogurt

fresh coriander or mint sprigs

❶ Heat the vegetable oil in a large saucepan and sauté the onion and apple for 3–4 minutes. Add the garlic, carrot, parsnip and curry paste and cook, stirring, for 1 more minute.

❷ Add the chicken to the saucepan and cook for 2–3 minutes, stirring often, until sealed.

❸ Add the chicken stock, sultanas and chopped coriander or mint to the saucepan, stirring well. Bring up to simmering point and then partially cover and reduce the heat. Cook over a low heat for about 40 minutes.

❹ About 15 minutes before the end of cooking time, cook the rice in plenty of lightly salted boiling water for about 12 minutes, until tender. Drain thoroughly and rinse with boiling water.

❺ Slice the banana and stir it into the curry. Check the seasoning, adding salt and pepper, according to taste.

❻ Serve the curry with the hot, cooked rice. Top each portion with 1 tablespoon of yogurt and garnish with fresh coriander or mint.

VARIATION Try using a Balti curry paste for a change. The **POINTS** values per serving will remain the same. Instead of serving the yogurt plain, add about 2 tablespoons of finely chopped cucumber to make a refreshing raita.

 **Fish and chips**

(7 POINTS VALUE)

Takes 15 minutes to prepare, 50 minutes to cook

| serves **4** | ***POINTS*** values per recipe **28** | calories per serving **400** |

Instead of frying – which adds fat and ***POINTS*** values – try this oven baked version of one of Britain's best loved dishes.

2 tablespoons olive oil
700 g (1 lb 9 oz) unpeeled potatoes, scrubbed and cut into wedges
4 x 175 g (6 oz) cod or haddock fillets
2 tablespoons plain white flour
1 egg
50 g (1¾ oz) dried breadcrumbs
salt and freshly ground black pepper
malt vinegar or lemon wedges, to serve

❶ Preheat the oven to Gas Mark 6/200°C/fan oven 180°C. Grease a roasting pan and a baking sheet with 1 teaspoon of the oil. Heat the roasting pan in the oven for 5 minutes.

❷ Put the potato wedges in the roasting pan and sprinkle them with the remaining oil. Toss them together and then season with salt and pepper. Bake for about 30 minutes, until barely tender.

❸ Meanwhile, rinse the fish fillets and pat them dry with kitchen paper. Sprinkle the flour on a plate, and season it with salt and pepper. Coat the fish fillets in the seasoned flour.

❹ Beat the egg in a shallow bowl with 2 tablespoons of cold water. Sprinkle the breadcrumbs on a separate plate. Dip the floured fish fillets in the egg and then coat them in the breadcrumbs. Place the fillets on the prepared baking sheet.

❺ Reduce the oven temperature to Gas Mark 5/190°C/fan oven 170°C and continue to bake the potatoes, with the fish positioned on the shelf below them, for a further 15–20 minutes. Check that the fish is cooked by testing it with a fork; the flesh should be opaque and flake easily.

❻ Serve the fish with the oven baked wedges, seasoned with vinegar or lemon, salt and pepper.

VARIATION Try using coley or haddock instead of cod. They are more economical and will reduce the ***POINTS*** values to 6½ per serving.

(2) Spicy fish burgers

Takes 25 minutes

| serves **4** | **POINTS** values per recipe **7.5** | calories per serving **135** | ❄ |

Smoked fish tastes delicious in these burgers which take hardly any time to prepare and cook. Serve each burger with a crisp 0 **POINTS** value green salad and a medium size bun, adding 2 extra **POINTS** values.

300 g (10½ oz) skinless cod fillet
200 g (7 oz) skinless smoked cod fillet
1 small onion, chopped
1 teaspoon mild curry powder
low fat cooking spray
salt and freshly ground black pepper
1 lime, quartered, to serve

FOR THE CUCUMBER RELISH
¼ cucumber
150 g tub of low fat plain yogurt
1 tablespoon chopped fresh dill or ½ teaspoon dried dill
salt and freshly ground black pepper

❶ With your fingertips, check the fish for any bones and pull out any you can feel. Cut the flesh into chunks. Place the fish in a food processor with the onion, curry powder and half a teaspoon each of salt and pepper. Process the mixture in short bursts, scraping down the sides once or twice, until it becomes a chunky paste – don't over process it.

❷ Divide the mixture into four smooth balls, and then flatten them into burger shapes. Chill them in the refrigerator until required.

❸ Meanwhile, make the relish. Halve the cucumber and scoop out the seeds with a teaspoon. Chop the flesh finely or coarsely grate it. Mix it with the yogurt, dill and seasoning. Chill the relish in the refrigerator until you need it.

❹ When you are ready to cook the burgers, heat a large non stick frying pan and spray it with low fat cooking spray. Add the burgers to the pan and cook them for about 3–4 minutes on each side, turning them carefully, until golden brown and firm when pressed.

❺ Serve the fish burgers with a lime quarter for each serving and the cucumber relish.

TOP TIP Open freeze these burgers and then store in plastic bags in the freezer. That way they won't stick together and can be eaten one at a time.

VARIATION Any smoked or white fish works well in these burgers, e.g. haddock, whiting or hake, but remember to alter the **POINTS** values accordingly.

 **Sticky ribs**

Takes 10 minutes to prepare, 1 hour to cook

serves **4**   *POINTS* values per recipe **22**   calories per serving **355**

Chinese style pork spare ribs make a very tasty starter – or you could serve them as a main meal with 4 tablespoons of boiled rice, adding an extra 3 *POINTS* values per serving.

500 g (1 lb 2 oz) pork spare ribs
4 tablespoons tomato purée
2 tablespoons rice vinegar or cider vinegar
2 tablespoons soy sauce
2 tablespoons hoisin sauce
1 teaspoon Chinese five spice powder
2 teaspoons light or dark muscovado sugar
salt and freshly ground black pepper

TO SERVE
1 tablespoon chopped fresh coriander or parsley
2 spring onions, sliced finely

❶ Preheat the oven to Gas Mark 6/200°C/fan oven 180°C.

❷ Put the spare ribs into a large roasting pan.

❸ In a bowl, mix together the tomato purée, rice or cider vinegar, soy sauce, hoisin sauce, five spice powder and sugar. Season with salt and pepper and brush this mixture generously over the ribs to glaze them.

❹ Roast the ribs for 30 minutes, then baste them again with the leftover glazing mixture, adding any remaining mixture to the roasting pan. Roast the ribs for a further 20–25 minutes.

❺ Serve the ribs, sprinkled with the chopped coriander or parsley and sliced spring onions.

VARIATION 1 Substitute oyster sauce for the hoisin sauce if you prefer. The *POINTS* values will be reduced to 5 per serving.

VARIATION 2 For extra bite, add a teaspoon or two of hot chilli sauce to the glaze mixture. The *POINTS* values will remain the same.

(3) Turkey stroganoff

Takes 25 minutes

serves **4**   *POINTS* values per recipe **12.5**   calories per serving **185**

This is lovely served with rice and some fresh watercress. Don't forget to add the extra *POINTS* values for the rice.

garlic low fat cooking spray
450 g (1 lb) prepared turkey stir fry strips
1 onion, chopped finely
200 g (7 oz) mushrooms, sliced
6 tablespoons half fat crème fraîche
100 ml (3½ fl oz) skimmed milk
2 teaspoons Dijon mustard
salt and freshly ground black pepper
paprika, to garnish

❶ Using a non stick pan and the low fat cooking spray, fry the turkey strips until browned.

❷ Add the onion and mushrooms and continue to fry until cooked.

❸ Add the rest of ingredients and stir well to form a sauce. Heat through and serve with a sprinkling of paprika on top to add some colour.

(5½) Boston baked beans

Takes 10 minutes to prepare, 2 hours to cook

serves **4**   *POINTS* values per recipe **23**   calories per serving **415**

Begin this recipe the night before, by soaking the beans overnight.

200 g (7 oz) haricot beans, soaked overnight
1 onion, chopped finely
2 tablespoons brown sugar
2 tablespoons black treacle
1 tablespoon whole grain mustard
454 g packet of low fat sausages, each sausage cut into three

❶ Boil the beans for 10 minutes and then simmer for 30 minutes. Drain well.

❷ Meanwhile, preheat the oven to Gas Mark 4/180°C/fan oven 160°C.

❸ Mix the beans and all the other ingredients together and put into a casserole dish with 100 ml (3½ fl oz) boiling water. Cover and cook in the oven for 1 hour.

❹ Uncover and cook for 30 minutes more.

(4½ POINTS VALUE) Sausage and lentil casserole

Takes 15 minutes to prepare, 30 minutes to cook

| serves **4** | **_POINTS_** values per recipe **19** | calories per serving **325** | ❄ | **V*** |

*if using vegetarian sausages

How about preparing this recipe for Guy Fawkes night? It can be made well in advance, leaving you time to concentrate on other, noisier bangers on the night. Serve with a generous spoonful of mashed swede, which will not add any extra **_POINTS_** values.

450 g pack of 95% fat free pork sausages
1 large onion, chopped
1 garlic clove, crushed
1 large carrot, grated coarsely
175 g (6 oz) Puy lentils
fresh thyme, to taste
400 g can of chopped tomatoes
600 ml (1 pint) hot beef stock
4 tablespoons half fat crème fraîche
salt and freshly ground black pepper

❶ Prick the sausages all over, then dry fry in a non stick saucepan, until lightly coloured. Add the onion to the pan and continue to stir fry until the onion is softened and golden. Add the garlic and carrot and cook for a further minute.

❷ Stir in the lentils, thyme sprigs, chopped tomatoes and stock. Bring to the boil, then reduce the heat to a gentle simmer and cook, uncovered, for 30 minutes. Stir occasionally, adding a drop of water if the mixture becomes too dry. Season to taste.

❸ When the casserole is ready to serve, stir in the crème fraîche.

TOP TIP Try Puy lentils, which you will find in good supermarkets. They require no soaking and taste great! Otherwise, green lentils or continental lentils are a good substitute.

VARIATION For a vegetarian option, use 2 x 250 g packs of Quorn sausages and vegetatable stock. Replace the beef stock with a good quality vegetable stock. The **_POINTS_** values per serving will be 5½.

(4) Rustic bolognese

Takes 15 minutes to prepare, 35 minutes to cook

serves **4**   *POINTS* values per recipe **16.5**   calories per serving **330**

This version is much lower in *POINTS* values than the traditional family favourite – but no one would ever guess!

low fat cooking spray
1 green pepper, de-seeded and diced
1 onion, diced
1 garlic clove, chopped
225 g (8 oz) extra lean beef mince
1 courgette, diced
1 large carrot, diced
150 g (3½ oz) chestnut mushrooms
400 g can of chopped tomatoes
2 tablespoons tomato purée
1 tablespoon chopped fresh marjoram
180 g (6½ oz) dried spaghetti
salt and freshly ground black pepper
2 tablespoons chopped fresh basil, to serve

1 Spray a large saucepan with low fat cooking spray and add the green pepper, onion and garlic. Fry for 3–4 minutes, stirring occasionally, until they start to soften.

2 Add the minced beef and fry for a further 6–8 minutes to brown the meat, stirring from time to time.

3 Add the courgette, carrot, mushrooms, canned tomatoes, tomato purée, marjoram and seasoning. Stir well before adding 200 ml (7 fl oz) of water. Stir again and bring to a simmer. Simmer for 20 minutes.

4 Bring a large saucepan of lightly salted water to the boil. Add the spaghetti and cook for 10–12 minutes until just tender.

5 Drain the spaghetti and divide between four warmed plates or pasta bowls and spoon over the Bolognese sauce. Sprinkle with the chopped basil and serve immediately.

VARIATION Try using chicken or turkey mince for a change. The *POINTS* values per serving will be 3½.

Roast chicken with autumn fruits

Takes 10 minutes to prepare, 35 minutes to cook

serves **4**   *POINTS* values per recipe **15.5**   calories per serving **255**

Chicken is coated in sage and apple seasoning, then roasted with apples and pears. This is a great recipe for the whole family and ideal for Sunday lunch.

25 g (1 oz) plain flour
2 teaspoons sage and apple seasoning (or use dried mixed herbs)
4 medium skinless, boneless chicken breasts
1 tablespoon olive oil
2 apples
1 pear
1 tablespoon lemon juice
salt and freshly ground black pepper

❶ Preheat the oven to Gas Mark 5/190°C/fan oven 170°C.

❷ Sprinkle the flour on to a plate and add the sage and apple seasoning or mixed herbs. Season with salt and pepper and mix well.

❸ Rinse the chicken breasts, but do not pat dry. Roll in the seasoned flour. Place in a roasting tin, sprinkle with the oil, transfer to the oven and cook for 15 minutes.

❹ Quarter and core the apples and pear, without peeling them. Sprinkle with lemon juice and place them next to the chicken. Roast for a further 20 minutes, or until the chicken is cooked and the fruit is tender.

VARIATION 1 Use garlic flavoured olive oil if you like; it adds a delicious taste to the chicken.

VARIATION 2 If you want to use a medium whole chicken, in step two, brush the chicken with olive oil and then roll in the seasoned flour. Sprinkle the chicken with 1 teaspoon of oil and then cook in the oven for 1 hour. The *POINTS* values will remain the same for a 150 g (5½ oz) portion of chicken.

(7) Chicken pot pie

Takes 10 minutes to prepare, 20 minutes to cook

serves **4**   *POINTS* values per recipe **27.5**   calories per serving **235**   ❄

This recipe makes for a wonderful and warming family meal, and will satisfy you even on the hungriest of days.

2 teaspoons low fat spread

500 g (1 lb 2 oz) skinless, boneless chicken thighs, trimmed of fat and halved lengthways

1 carrot, sliced thinly

1 parsnip, chopped

1 celery stick, sliced thinly

1 leek, sliced thinly

1 large potato, scrubbed and chopped

½ teaspoon dried thyme

1 large bay leaf

1 teaspoon coarse grain mustard

2 teaspoons plain white flour

300 ml (½ pint) chicken or vegetable stock

salt and freshly ground black pepper

❶ Melt the low fat spread in a cast iron casserole dish and sauté the chicken thigh pieces for about 3 minutes until browned.

❷ Stir in the vegetables and 4 tablespoons of water. Cover and simmer for 5 minutes until the vegetables have softened. Mix in the thyme and bay leaf, and then add the mustard and flour, stirring well to blend them in. Stir in the stock. Season and bring the pan to the boil.

❸ Reduce the heat, cover and simmer for 15 minutes until the meat and vegetables are tender. Serve on four warmed plates.

TOP TIP Mild and coarse grain mustard are great in sauces; they add a subtle bite without adding extra *POINTS* values. Dijon mustards have a lovely, tangy flavour.

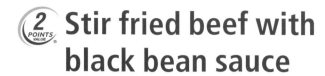 # Stir fried beef with black bean sauce

Takes 10 minutes to prepare, 15–20 minutes to cook

serves **4**   *POINTS* values per recipe **8.5**   calories per serving **155**

Stir frying is so quick, and with lots of great sauces available it's the perfect way to make a delicious low *POINTS* values meal. Serve with steamed pak choi.

low fat cooking spray
300 g (10½ oz) lean beef fillet steak, cut into small bite size pieces
1 onion, sliced
2 garlic cloves, crushed
2 cm (¾ inch) piece of fresh root ginger, peeled and chopped
1 yellow pepper, de-seeded and sliced
150 g (5½ oz) green beans, cut in half
4 tablespoons black bean sauce

❶ Heat a wok or large frying pan and spray with low fat cooking spray. Add the pieces of beef and stir fry for 5–6 minutes, until browned. Remove with a slotted spoon.

❷ To the wok, add the onion, garlic and ginger and stir fry for 4–5 minutes before adding the pepper and green beans. Stir fry for another 2–3 minutes.

❸ Return the beef to the wok with the black bean sauce and 100 ml (3½ fl oz) of water.

❹ Stir fry for another 5–6 minutes, until the beef is cooked and the sauce has thickened.

TOP TIP For stir frying, always make sure your wok or frying pan is quite hot before adding the first ingredient.

VARIATION For a 0 *POINTS* value vegetarian version, omit the beef and replace with 300 g (10½ oz) 0 *POINTS* value vegetables of your choice, e.g. courgette, broccoli and red pepper, all sliced thinly.

Teriyaki beef with ginger noodles

Takes 35 minutes

serves **2**   **POINTS** values per recipe **14**   calories per serving **475**   ✳

When you feel like spoiling yourself with fillet steak, this succulent dish fits the bill perfectly!

125 g (4½ oz) medium egg noodles
225 g (8 oz) fillet steak
3 tablespoons Teriyaki sauce
1 tablespoon tomato purée
1 garlic clove, crushed
1 tablespoon sherry
2 teaspoons sunflower oil
2.5 cm (1 inch) piece of root ginger, peeled and chopped finely
150 g (5½ oz) shiitake mushrooms, halved
100 g (3½ oz) canned bamboo shoots, drained
3 spring onions, sliced into long, thin strips

❶ Place the noodles in a bowl and pour over boiling water. Leave them to stand for 15 minutes.

❷ Meanwhile, slice the steak as thinly as you can. Place the beef slices in a shallow dish with the Teriyaki sauce, tomato purée, garlic and sherry. Mix well so that the steak slices are evenly coated in the mixture. Leave the meat for 10 minutes to marinate.

❸ Heat the sunflower oil in a non stick frying pan or wok. Drain the beef, reserving any marinade, and add it to the pan with the ginger. Stir fry for 2 minutes and then add the mushrooms, bamboo shoots, most of the spring onions and the reserved marinade.

❹ Drain the noodles and add them to the pan. Mix them in well and heat through for 2–3 minutes. Serve at once, sprinkled with the remaining spring onions.

⑤½ POINTS VALUE Mediterranean risotto

Takes 40 minutes

serves **2**	**POINTS** values per recipe **11**	calories per serving **330**		**V**

The secret of a successful risotto is to choose the right variety of rice, and then be patient as it slowly absorbs the stock to become creamy and delicious.

15 g (½ oz) sun dried tomatoes
2 teaspoons olive oil
100 g (3½ oz) Arborio or risotto rice
1 small onion, chopped
1 small garlic clove, crushed
1 celery stick, sliced
½ red or yellow pepper, de-seeded and chopped
175 g (6 oz) mixed mushrooms, sliced
50 ml (2 fl oz) dry white wine
1 vegetable stock cube, dissolved in 425 ml (15 fl oz) hot water
1 tablespoon chopped fresh herbs (basil, oregano, marjoram, chives or parsley)
2 tablespoons finely grated Parmesan cheese
salt and freshly ground black pepper

❶ Put the tomatoes in a bowl and pour over enough boiling water to just cover them. Leave them to soak for 20 minutes.

❷ Meanwhile, heat the oil in a heavy based frying pan or saucepan. Add the rice and gently sauté it, without browning, for about 5 minutes. Add the onion, garlic, celery, pepper and mushrooms. Cook over a very low heat, stirring, for 2–3 more minutes.

❸ Pour in the wine, allowing it to bubble up for a few moments, and then add about a quarter of the hot stock and bring to the boil. Reduce the heat and simmer gently, stirring occasionally, for about 10 minutes. Ladle in more stock as needed and cook until the rice is almost tender.

❹ Drain the tomatoes, adding the soaking liquid to the rice. Tear the tomatoes into pieces and add them to the risotto with any remaining stock. Cook gently until the liquid has been absorbed and the rice is tender.

❺ Add the herbs and half the Parmesan cheese to the risotto. Season with salt and pepper and serve at once, sprinkled with the remaining cheese.

TOP TIP Add a little extra stock or water if the rice is not fully cooked after it has absorbed all the liquid.

VARIATION Leave the pepper out if you're not keen on its flavour, or replace it with a chopped courgette. The **POINTS** values will remain the same.

Macaroni cheese

Takes 10 minutes to prepare, 20 minutes to cook

serves **4**   *POINTS* values per recipe **28.5**   calories per serving **415**   ❄   **V**

Why not just have half a portion of this macaroni cheese for a light meal to reduce the *POINTS* values per serving to 4? Serve with a large green salad tossed in fat free dressing for no extra *POINTS* values and you'll still feel full.

175 g (6 oz) macaroni or pasta tubes
25 g (1 oz) polyunsaturated margarine
40 g (1½ oz) plain white flour
450 ml (16 fl oz) skimmed milk
100 g (3½ oz) extra mature Cheddar cheese, grated
1 heaped teaspoon wholegrain mustard
4 tomatoes, sliced
1 slice of bread from a large thick sliced loaf, cut into cubes
salt and freshly ground black pepper

❶ Cook the macaroni or pasta tubes in a large saucepan of lightly salted, boiling water for about 10–12 minutes until just tender, or follow the pack instructions.

❷ Meanwhile, make an all in one sauce by putting the margarine, flour and milk into a medium saucepan. Heat, stirring all the time with a small wire whisk, until the sauce boils and thickens. Reduce the heat and cook gently for another minute. Remove from the heat and add most of the cheese, reserving a little for the topping. Let it melt in the heat of the sauce.

❸ Preheat the grill to a medium high heat and warm a 1.5 litre (2¾ pint) heatproof dish.

❹ Add the mustard to the sauce and season with salt and pepper. Drain the macaroni thoroughly and add it to the warmed dish. Pour over the cheese sauce, stirring it into the macaroni.

❺ Arrange the tomatoes over the top of the macaroni cheese. Scatter the bread cubes and reserved cheese over the surface. Grill for about 5 minutes until bubbling and golden brown.

VARIATION You don't have to use macaroni – just use your own favourite pasta, though a shape which holds sauce well works best.

(5½ POINTS VALUE) Traditional fish pie

Takes 20 minutes to prepare, 1 hour to cook

serves **4**   *POINTS* values per recipe **22**   calories per serving **390**   ❄

Fish pie is so delicious and it's a dish that all the family will enjoy. Serve with plenty of 0 *POINTS* value vegetables, such as carrots, broccoli or green beans.

700 g (1 lb 9 oz) potatoes, peeled
2 large leeks, chopped
300 ml (½ pint) plus 2 tablespoons skimmed milk
1 tablespoon chopped fresh parsley or chives, plus extra, to garnish
25 g (1 oz) polyunsaturated margarine
50 g (1¾ oz) plain white flour
450 g (1 lb) skinned and boned cod, cut into chunks
100 g (3½ oz) frozen, peeled prawns, defrosted
50 g (1¾ oz) frozen peas, defrosted
salt and freshly ground black pepper

❶ Cook the potatoes in boiling, lightly salted water until just tender. Meanwhile, cook the leeks in a small amount of lightly salted boiling water for about 5 minutes. Drain them both well, reserving the cooking liquid.

❷ Mash the potatoes, adding 2 tablespoons of milk. Make the remaining 300 ml (½ pint) of milk up to 450 ml (16 fl oz) with the cooking liquid from the potatoes and leeks. Add the chopped parsley or chives.

❸ Put the margarine, flour and milk mixture into a saucepan. Heat, stirring constantly with a small wire whisk or wooden spoon, until thickened and smooth. Check the seasoning, adding salt and pepper if necessary.

❹ Preheat the oven to Gas Mark 5/190°C/fan oven 170°C.

❺ Put the cod in the base of a 1.2 litre (2 pint) baking dish and scatter the cooked leeks, prawns and peas on top. Pour over the sauce. Pipe or spoon the mashed potato over the surface.

❻ Bake in the oven for 30–35 minutes until cooked and browned, then serve, sprinkled with more chopped parsley or chives.

Garlic and rosemary leg of lamb

Takes 10 minutes to prepare + marinating, 1½ hours to cook + 15 minutes standing.

serves **4**   *POINTS* values per recipe **25.5**   calories per serving **465**   ❄

A perfect Sunday lunch treat served with freshly cooked veggies.

½ leg of lamb (about 1 kg/2 lb 4 oz in weight)
4 garlic cloves, sliced
8 small sprigs of fresh rosemary
1 orange, cut into thin slices
1 tablespoon clear honey
salt and freshly ground black pepper

❶ Rinse the lamb and pat dry. Lift into a shallow non metallic dish.

❷ Make random slits all over the top of the lamb and insert slices of garlic and rosemary sprigs. Arrange the orange slices over the top and season well. Cover and leave to marinate for at least 3 hours or preferably overnight.

❸ Preheat the oven to Gas Mark 6/200°C/fan oven 180°C. Lift the lamb into a roasting tin, removing the orange slices and cook for 1 hour. Brush the top with honey and return to the oven for 30 minutes. Allow to stand for 15 minutes before carving.

(6) Plum and banana crumble

Takes 10 minutes to prepare, 40 minutes to cook

| serves **4** | **POINTS** values per recipe **25** | calories per serving **395** | | V |

If you have the **POINTS** values to spare, serve this favourite with steaming hot, ready to serve, low fat custard for an extra 2 **POINTS** values per serving.

FOR THE FILLING

600 g (1 lb 5 oz) ripe Victoria plums, halved and stoned

2 large bananas, cut on to 2.5 cm (1 inch) chunks

1 tablespoon light soft brown sugar or caster sugar

FOR THE CRUMBLE

125 g (4½ oz) plain flour

½ teaspoon ground cinnamon or mixed spice

75 g (2¾ oz) half fat butter

2 tablespoons demerara sugar

50 g (1¾ oz) porridge oats

❶ Preheat the oven to Gas Mark 4/180°C/fan oven 160°C.

❷ Prepare the filling. Mix the plums, bananas and sugar together. Transfer to a 850 ml (1½ pint) ovenproof dish. Spoon 4 tablespoons of water over the fruit mixture.

❸ To make the crumble, place the flour, spice, low fat spread and the sugar in a bowl. Rub together until the mixture resembles coarse breadcrumbs. Stir in the oats.

❹ Sprinkle the topping over the fruit, making sure it is completely covered. Transfer to a baking sheet and cook for 40 minutes, or until golden and bubbling at the edges. Leave to cool slightly before serving.

TOP TIP A food processor makes light work of the crumble mixture. Simply tip all the ingredients into the bowl and process for about 10 seconds .

VARIATION For a change, replace the plums with firm pears, peeled and quartered.

Steamed chocolate castles

Takes 10 minutes to prepare + standing, 15–20 minutes to cook

| serves **6** | **POINTS** values per recipe **31.5** | calories per serving **315** | ❄ | **V** |

Invest in some small moulds or ramekin dishes to make these little puddings. They will become a huge success with the whole family. Crown the tops with the delicious vanilla sauce.

low fat cooking spray
75 g (2¾ oz) dark chocolate (minimum 70% cocoa solids)
150 ml (¼ pint) skimmed milk
150 g (5½ oz) Madeira sponge cake, crumbled
50 g (1¾ oz) low fat spread
50 g (1¾ oz) caster sugar
2 eggs, separated
2 drops of vanilla essence

FOR THE SAUCE
2 level tablespoons sauce flour
1 tablespoon caster sugar
425 ml (¾ pint) skimmed milk
a few drops of vanilla essence

❶ Lightly spray six moulds or 8 cm (3 inch) ramekin dishes with the low fat cooking spray.

❷ Place the chocolate into a saucepan with the milk and heat gently until melted. Stir, then bring to the boil. Pour the chocolate mixture over the cake crumbs and leave to stand for 20 minutes.

❸ Put the low fat spread and sugar into a small bowl and beat together until light and creamy. Beat in the egg yolks, vanilla essence and cake crumb mixture. Whisk the egg whites until stiff then carefully fold into the mixture. Divide between the moulds or ramekin dishes, cover with a piece of greaseproof paper and place in a steamer (see **Variation 1** if you do not have a steamer). Steam for 15–20 minutes or until lightly set.

❺ To make the sauce, blend the flour and sugar with a little of the milk to a smooth paste in a small saucepan. Whisk in the remaining milk and stir over a moderate heat until the sauce comes to a boil. Allow the sauce to boil for 1 minute, stirring all the time as it becomes thick and smooth. Remove from the heat then stir in the vanilla essence.

❻ Turn the steamed puddings out on to individual plates and drizzle the sauce over the top.

TOP TIP Steaming is the healthiest method of cooking. Not only is it quick but also, when cooking vegetables and fruit, it preserves a high proportion of nutrients compared to other conventional methods. The flavours and textures of all steamed food are superb too. You will find that most steaming recipes are naturally low in fat, which has to be good!

VARIATION 1 If you do not have a steamer, cover and cook in a preheated oven (Gas Mark 6/200°C/fan oven 180°C) in a roasting tin filled with 2.5 cm (1 inch) of water for 15–20 minutes.

VARIATION 2 For a creamier sauce, stir in 2 tablespoons of half fat crème fraîche. The **POINTS** values per serving will be the same.

(3½ POINTS VALUE) Saturday sundaes

Takes 15 minutes + setting

serves **4**	**POINTS** values per recipe **14**	calories per serving **155**	**V**

The perfect weekend treat – fresh fruit chunks layered with fruit sauce, low fat custard and chopped jelly – with squirty cream and a cherry on the top!

1 packet of strawberry or raspberry sugar free jelly crystals
350 g (12 oz) strawberries or raspberries
powdered sweetener, to taste
1 banana, sliced
1 kiwi fruit, peeled and sliced
1 peach or nectarine, peeled and chopped
2 x 150 g pots of low fat, ready to serve custard
4 tablespoons aerosol cream
4 glacé cherries

❶ Make up the sugar free jelly according to pack instructions and leave to set.

❷ Purée half the strawberries or raspberries in a liquidiser or blender. Alternatively, mash them or push them through a sieve. Add a little powdered sweetener, to taste.

❸ Chop the jelly and divide between four sundae glasses. Mix the remaining strawberries or raspberries with the rest of the fruit, and layer in the glasses with the custard and strawberry or raspberry purée.

❹ Squirt 1 tablespoon of cream on to each dessert, then pop a glacé cherry on the top.

VARIATION For a quick dessert that's very simple to make, substitute a 410 g can of fruit cocktail in grape or natural juice and use instead of banana, kiwi and peach or nectarine. The **POINTS** values per serving will be 3.

(6½ POINTS VALUE) Black cherry and cinnamon crumble

Takes 25 minutes to prepare, 25 minutes to bake

serves **4**	**POINTS** values per recipe **27**	calories per serving **435**	❋	**V**

Mixing cherries with the traditional apple gives this dish a unique flavour and texture.

350 g (12 oz) cooking apples, peeled, cored and diced
425 g (15 oz) canned cherries in juice, stoned
1 tablespoon arrowroot

FOR THE CRUMBLE
150 g (5½ oz) plain white flour
1 teaspoon ground cinnamon
75 g (2¾ oz) polyunsaturated margarine
50 g (1¾ oz) demerara sugar

❶ Preheat the oven to Gas Mark 5/190°C/fan oven 170°C.

❷ Place the apples in a large saucepan with the canned cherries and juice, and heat until just boiling.

❸ Mix the arrowroot with a little cold water to make a thin paste and stir this into the pan. Cook, stirring, until the juices thicken slightly. Spoon the fruit mixture into an ovenproof dish.

❹ Sift the flour and cinnamon into a mixing bowl. Rub in the margarine using your fingertips, until the mixture resembles fine breadcrumbs. Stir in the sugar and then scatter the crumble over the top of the fruit.

❺ Bake for 25 minutes, until the crumble topping is crunchy and golden. Serve hot or cold.

TOP TIP Look out for a good low fat custard to serve with this, or better still make your own with custard powder, skimmed milk and granulated artificial sweetener. Don't forget to alter the **POINTS** values accordingly.

 **Blackberry fool**

Takes 10 minutes + 1 hour chilling

serves **4**	**POINTS** values per recipe **5**	calories per serving **80**	**V**

Those with a sweet tooth can add 2 teaspoons of caster sugar when they add the custard and yogurt; this will add ½ a **POINTS** value per serving.

400 g (14 oz) blackberries
200 g carton of low fat ready to serve custard
100 g (3½ oz) 0% fat Greek yogurt

❶ Purée the fruit roughly.

❷ Mix in the custard and yogurt.

❸ Spoon into a serving bowl or four individual bowls.

❹ Chill for 1 hour before serving.

VARIATION You can substitute raspberries for the blackberries.

(3½ POINTS VALUE) Ginger puddings

Takes 10 minutes to prepare, 30 minutes to cook

serves **4**   *POINTS* values per recipe **14.5**   calories per serving **230**   ✳   **V**

These are delicious served with ice cream or a little golden syrup thinned with hot water. Adjust the *POINTS* values accordingly.

80 g (3 oz) self raising flour
½ teaspoon ground ginger
¼ teaspoon ground cinnamon
¼ teaspoon baking powder
¼ teaspoon bicarbonate of soda
1 egg, beaten
8 teaspoons corn oil
40 g (1½ oz) soft brown sugar
2 teaspoons golden syrup

❶ Preheat the oven to Gas Mark 5/190°C/fan oven 170°C Have ready four 150 ml (¼ pint) pudding basins (tin, glass or foil).

❷ Sift the dry ingredients into a bowl and then whisk in the rest of the ingredients. Add 75 ml (3 fl oz) warm water.

❸ Divide between the pudding basins and place on a baking tray.

❹ Bake in the preheated oven for 25–30 minutes, until firm to the touch.

❺ Cool in the basins for 5 minutes and then loosen with a knife and turn out.

Lazy lasagne

Takes 35 minutes to prepare, 40 minutes to cook

serves **4**   **POINTS** values per recipe **27**   calories per serving **585**   ❄

As delicious as lasagne can be, it is still fairly time consuming to make. For this recipe, labour saving products have been used to produce a satisfying lasagne in minutes. Serve with a crisp green salad for no extra **POINTS** values.

low fat cooking spray
400 g (14 oz) lean minced beef
1 tablespoon Worcestershire sauce
520 g jar low fat ragu Bolognese sauce
200 g (7 oz) button mushrooms, sliced in half
150 g (5½ oz) no precook lasagne sheets

FOR THE SAUCE
300 ml (½ pint) skimmed milk
1 bouquet garni sachet
3 tablespoons cornflour
50 g (1¾ oz) mature, reduced fat Cheddar cheese
2 teaspoons French mustard
salt and freshly ground black pepper

❶ Preheat the oven to Gas Mark 5/190°C/fan oven 170°C. Heat a large, non stick frying pan and spray with the low fat cooking spray. Fry the meat until it is not longer pink and the grains are separated, stirring, then season and add the Worcestershire sauce, ragu and mushrooms. Bring to the boil. Simmer for a few minutes.

❷ Meanwhile, make the cheese sauce by simmering all but 2 tablespoons of the milk with the bouquet garni for 5 minutes. Remove the bouquet garni and blend the cornflour with the remaining milk and add to the hot milk. Bring back to the boil and cook for a further 2 minutes until thickened, stirring. Season, then add the cheese and mustard and stir again.

❸ Put a layer of mince in the base of an ovenproof dish, cover with a layer of lasagne sheets, then a layer of mince. Repeat until you have used up all the lasagne and mince. Pour the cheese sauce over and bake for 40 minutes until golden and tender when tested with the point of a sharp knife.

⑤½ Goat's cheese salad

Takes 25 minutes

serves 4	POINTS values per recipe 22.5	calories per serving 300		V

Melted cheese on toast makes this a very special salad.

150 g (5½ oz) French stick, cut into 2.5 cm (1 inch) slices
low fat cooking spray
150 g (5½ oz) goat's cheese, sliced thinly
225 g (8 oz) fine green beans
2 Little Gem lettuces, shredded
150 g (5½ oz) baby spinach leaves
salt and freshly ground black pepper

FOR THE DRESSING
1 teaspoon white wine vinegar
1 teaspoon caster sugar
1 teaspoon sesame oil

❶ Preheat the oven to Gas Mark 5/190°C/fan oven 170°C.
Spray each slice of French stick with a little low fat cooking
spray and bake in the oven for 5 minutes until crunchy.

❷ Top the bread with the goat's cheese slices and return to
the oven for 5 minutes, until the cheese begins to melt.

❸ Meanwhile, cook the beans in lightly salted, boiling water
for 2 minutes. Drain and refresh them under cold running
water. Toss them together with the lettuce and spinach.

❹ Mix together the dressing ingredients and drizzle this
over the salad. Toss everything thoroughly and then divide
the salad between four plates. Top the salad with the goat's
cheese toasts and a generous grinding of black pepper.

TOP TIP If you want to add a little colour to the salad, add
225 g (8 oz) halved cherry tomatoes or a thinly sliced, de-
seeded red pepper. The POINTS values will remain the same.

③ Luxury cauliflower cheese

Takes 35 minutes

serves 4	POINTS values per recipe 12.5	calories per serving 220	❄	V

225 g (8 oz) leeks, sliced
175 g (6 oz) carrots, diced
450 g (1 lb) cauliflower, broken into florets
100 g (3½ oz) frozen peas
300 ml (10 fl oz) skimmed milk
200 g (7 oz) low fat soft cheese
25 g (1 oz) cornflour
25 g (1 oz) half fat Cheddar cheese, grated
15 g (½ oz) fresh wholemeal breadcrumbs
2 teaspoons olive oil
salt and freshly ground black pepper

❶ Cook the leeks, carrots and cauliflower in a large saucepan
of lightly salted, boiling water for 5 minutes. Add the peas to
the pan and cook for a further 5 minutes. Drain well.

❷ Meanwhile, gently heat the milk and low fat soft cheese
together, whisking until smooth. Mix the cornflour with a
little cold water to make a thin paste. When the milk and
cheese mixture is almost boiling, add the cornflour paste
and cook, stirring, until you have a thick and smooth sauce.
Season to taste.

❸ Transfer the drained vegetables to a flameproof dish
and pour over the sauce. Mix together the grated cheese,
breadcrumbs and olive oil, and sprinkle over the top. Grill
under a medium heat for 2–3 minutes until the topping is
bubbling and golden. Serve at once.

Cheese, onion and tomato quiche

Takes 20 minutes to prepare, 30 minutes to cook

| serves **4** | *POINTS* values per recipe **19.5** | calories per serving **350** | ❄ | **V** |

Filo pastry gives a new slant to an old favourite, and helps to keep the *POINTS* values under control. Serve with a large, mixed salad with fat free dressing for no extra *POINTS* values.

FOR THE PASTRY
8 sheets of fresh filo pastry
2 tablespoons delicately flavoured or light olive oil

FOR THE FILLING
2 teaspoons olive oil
2 large onions, sliced into rings
3 large tomatoes, sliced
2 eggs
150 ml (¼ pint) skimmed milk
1 tablespoon chopped fresh mixed herbs, or 1 teaspoon dried mixed herbs
40 g (1½ oz) mature Cheddar cheese, grated
salt and freshly ground black pepper

❶ Preheat the oven to Gas Mark 2/150°C/fan oven 130°C.

❷ Unroll the sheets of filo pastry, keeping them covered with clingfilm or a damp cloth as you work to prevent them drying out. Brush each one with a little olive oil and layer them in a 20 cm (8 inch) flan tin. Stand the flan tin on a baking sheet.

❸ For the filling, heat the oil in a frying pan and sauté the onions until softened, about 5 minutes. Tip them into the flan case and spread them over the base. Top with the sliced tomatoes.

❹ Beat together the eggs, milk and herbs. Season with salt and pepper and pour into the flan case. Sprinkle with the cheese and bake for 20–25 minutes on the middle shelf until set. Cool slightly before serving.

VARIATION If you're not keen on tomatoes, use a couple of sliced medium courgettes or 175 g (6 oz) of lightly cooked asparagus instead. The *POINTS* values per serving will remain the same.

(3) Classic fish soup with rouille

Takes 30 minutes to prepare, 45 minutes to cook

| serves **6** | **_POINTS_** values per recipe **18** | calories per serving **250** |

Enjoy this soup with a pungent garlic mayonnaise – a popular way to serve fish soup all over the Mediterranean. This soup is quite an elaborate affair and ideal for a special occasion.

1 kg (2 lb 4 oz) mixed fresh white fish, filleted heads and trimmings
   reserved (ask the fishmonger to include them)
250 g (9 oz) frozen uncooked prawns with their shells on, defrosted
   and peeled, shells reserved
a small bunch of parsley
1 bay leaf
2 onions, halved
low fat cooking spray
3 celery stalks, sliced
3 garlic cloves, crushed
400 g can of chopped tomatoes
1 strip of orange zest
1 tablespoon fennel seeds
1 tablespoon tomato purée
a pinch of saffron, soaked in 2 tablespoons boiling water (optional)
1 kg (2 lb 4 oz) mussels in their shells, washed and prepared
salt and freshly ground black pepper

FOR THE ROUILLE
2 garlic cloves, crushed
2 tablespoons low fat mayonnaise
juice of ½ a lemon

❶ Put all the fish trimmings and prawn shells in a large saucepan. Cover with 1.5 litres (2¾ pints) water and add the parsley stalks, bay leaf, one onion half and seasoning. Bring to the boil then simmer for 15 minutes. Strain and set aside, throwing away the shells and trimmings.

❷ Meanwhile, slice the remaining three onion halves. Heat a large non stick saucepan, spray with low fat cooking spray and stir fry the onion and celery for 5 minutes until softened. Add a little water if necessary to stop the mixture from sticking.

❸ Stir in the garlic, tomatoes, orange zest, fennel seeds, tomato purée and saffron with its soaking liquid, if using. Season to taste then add the strained fish stock and bring to the boil, cover and simmer for 20 minutes.

❹ Meanwhile, make the rouille by stirring together the garlic and mayonnaise with the lemon juice and seasoning.

❺ Add the fish to the pan and cook for 1 minute, then add the mussels and the prawns. Boil for another 4–5 minutes until the fish is opaque, the prawns pink and all the mussels are open, discarding any that remain closed.

❻ Chop the remaining parsley and scatter over the soup. Serve with a swirl of rouille on top of each serving.

TOP TIP Step 1 results in a delicious fish stock which can be used as a base for many fish soups and dishes but you can always use bought fish stock instead.

(4) Seafood paella

Takes 30 minutes to prepare, 20 minutes to cook

serves **4**   *POINTS* values per recipe **18**   calories per serving **350**

There are many varieties of this popular dish; this fish paella is a simplified version, but just as delicious.

1 teaspoon olive oil
1 small onion, chopped finely
1 garlic clove, crushed
5 saffron strands
2 tablespoons boiling water
1 red pepper, de-seeded and diced
225 g (8 oz) risotto rice
850 ml (1 ½ pints) fish or vegetable stock
125 g (4 ½ oz) frozen peas
225 g (8 oz) skinless cod fillet, cut into bite size pieces
125 g (4 ½ oz) peeled prawns
2 tablespoons chopped fresh parsley
salt and freshly ground black pepper

❶ Heat the olive oil in a frying pan and add the onion and garlic. Cook over a low heat, stirring until the onion has softened but not browned.

❷ Place the saffron in a small dish and cover with the boiling water. Leave to stand so the saffron infuses and colours the water a bright yellow.

❸ Add the red pepper and rice to the pan with the saffron and its soaking liquid and the stock. Bring to the boil and simmer for 15 minutes, until most of the liquid has been absorbed.

❹ Add the peas and fish and continue cooking for 5 minutes. Toss in the prawns and parsley, season to taste and cook for a further 2 to 3 minutes until piping hot.

(5) Salmon fishcakes

Takes 30 minutes to prepare + 20 minutes chilling

serves **4**   *POINTS* values per recipe **19.5**   calories per serving **325**

Serve with a fresh tomato and onion salad for no extra *POINTS* values.

300 g (10½ oz) fresh salmon, cooked or canned salmon, drained
300 g (10½ oz) potatoes, boiled in their skins then peeled and mashed
2 tablespoons parsley, chopped
2 eggs, beaten
2 tablespoons plain flour
75 g (2¾ oz) fresh breadcrumbs
low fat cooking spray
salt and freshly ground black pepper
chopped chives, to garnish

❶ Mix together the salmon, potato, parsley, seasoning and half the egg. Chill for at least 20 minutes.

❷ Place on a floured surface. Shape into a roll. Cut into 8 slices. Shape each one into a flat round, about 6 cm (2½ inches) in diameter and roll in the flour. Dip into the remaining egg, then coat in the breadcrumbs.

❸ Heat a frying pan and spray with the low fat cooking spray then fry the fish cakes for 2–3 minutes on each side or until golden brown and heated through. Garnish sprinkled with chives.

 Steak and kidney pie

Takes 20 minutes to prepare, 2¹/₂ hours to cook

| serves **6** | *POINTS* values per recipe **45** | calories per serving **390** | ❄ |

Mushrooms and sherry give a rich flavour to this classic British dish. If you don't eat any of the puff pastry topping, you'll be saving yourself 3½ *POINTS* values per serving.

2 teaspoons vegetable oil

700 g (1 lb 9 oz) lean stewing steak, cubed

2 x 25 g (1 oz) lamb's kidneys, trimmed and chopped

1 large onion, chopped

1 beef stock cube, dissolved in 450 ml (16 fl oz) hot water

2 tablespoons medium sherry

225 g (8 oz) mushrooms, sliced

1 tablespoon chopped fresh parsley

2 tablespoons cornflour, blended with 3–4 tablespoons cold water

225 g (8 oz) frozen puff pastry sheet, defrosted

1 tablespoon skimmed milk

salt and freshly ground black pepper

❶ Heat the oil in a large saucepan and over a high heat add the cubes of stewing steak a handful at a time, so that they seal and brown. Add the kidneys, stir well and then reduce the heat a little. Add the onion and cook for another 3–4 minutes, until softened.

❷ Add the stock, sherry, mushrooms and parsley to the saucepan. Bring up to the boil and then reduce the heat. Cover and simmer for 1½ hours, until the meat is very tender. Check the level of liquid from time to time, topping up with a little extra water if necessary.

❸ Preheat the oven to Gas Mark 7/220°C/fan oven 200°C.

❹ Season the cooked meat with salt and pepper. Add the blended cornflour and stir until thickened. Cook for 1 minute and then tip the mixture into an oblong baking dish.

❺ Lay the puff pastry sheet on top of the baking dish, trimming the edges with a sharp knife. Use the trimmings to make leaves for decoration. Position them on top, and brush the entire surface with milk. Bake for 25–30 minutes, until puffed up and golden brown.

 # Chicken balti

Takes 20 minutes to prepare, 20 minutes to cook

serves **4**   *POINTS* values per recipe **16**   calories per serving **260**

A mild, rich curry made with shop bought balti paste to speed up the preparation. The flavours and textures are far fresher and more interesting than the usual take away and there's the added advantage of far fewer *POINTS* values too. Serve with 4 tablespoons of cooked basmati rice and maybe 1 tablespoon of low fat plain yogurt, adding 3 extra *POINTS* values per serving.

low fat cooking spray
4 medium boneless, skinless chicken breasts, cubed
6 small new potatoes, quartered
1 onion, chopped finely
4 garlic cloves, crushed
5 cm (2 inch) piece of fresh root ginger, chopped finely
400 g can of chopped tomatoes
300 ml (½ pint) chicken stock
2 tablespoons balti curry paste
1 bunch of fresh coriander, chopped
salt and freshly ground black pepper
lemon wedges, to serve

❶ Heat a frying pan and spray with the low fat cooking spray, then stir fry the chicken for 4 minutes until golden round the edges and white all over. Add the potatoes, onion, garlic and ginger and fry for a further 4 minutes until turning golden.

❷ Add the tomatoes, stock and curry paste and bring to the boil. Simmer gently for 20 minutes until the chicken is tender and cooked through and the sauce has thickened.

❸ Stir in the coriander, adjust the seasoning if necessary, then serve with the lemon wedges.

 # Pasta arrabbiata

Takes 5 minutes to prepare, 15 minutes to cook

| serves **2** | ***POINTS*** values per recipe **11** | calories per serving **405** | ❄ |

This is a fast and fabulous version of the classic Italian recipe. It's wonderfully low in ***POINTS*** values and deliciously high in flavour.

2 rashers of lean smoked back bacon, trimmed of excess fat and
   chopped into strips
1 teaspoon olive oil
1 large garlic clove, chopped
½–1 teaspoon dried chilli flakes
400 g can of chopped tomatoes with herbs
150 g (5½ oz) pasta shapes or spaghetti
salt and freshly ground black pepper
1 tablespoon chopped fresh parsley, to serve

❶ Heat a non stick medium size saucepan until you can feel a good heat rising. Add the bacon and oil, and cook on a medium heat for 2 minutes.

❷ Add the garlic and enough chilli flakes to suit your taste, and then cook for a further 2 minutes. Stir in the tomatoes and seasoning, and cook for 10 minutes, stirring once or twice.

❸ Meanwhile, cook the pasta in lightly salted, boiling water for about 8 minutes or according to the pack instructions. Drain and then mix in the tomato and chilli sauce. Serve the pasta sprinkled with the parsley.

 # Moussaka

Takes 40 minutes to prepare, 1½ hours to cook

serves **4** **POINTS** values per recipe **20** calories per serving **315** ❄

A little time consuming to prepare but well worth the effort. Serve with a selection of freshly cooked vegetables or a green salad for a really satisfying meal.

225 g (8 oz) lean minced lamb
1 onion, chopped
1 garlic clove, crushed
1 teaspoon ground coriander
½ teaspoon ground cumin
1 teaspoon dried oregano
225 g (8 oz) courgettes, wiped and coarsely grated
150 ml (¼ pint) beef or lamb stock
1 aubergine
low fat cooking spray
350 g (12 oz) potatoes, peeled and sliced thinly
300 ml (½ pint) skimmed milk
2 tablespoons cornflour
100 g (3½ oz) low fat plain yogurt
a pinch of ground nutmeg
25 g (1 oz) fresh Parmesan cheese, grated
1 beefsteak tomato, sliced
salt and freshly ground black pepper

❶ Heat a non stick frying pan and add the mince. Dry fry until evenly browned and then drain off any excess fat. Add the onion, garlic, coriander, cumin, oregano and courgettes and cook for a further 5 minutes.

❷ Pour the stock over, season to taste. Cover and cook for 20 minutes, stirring from time to time.

❸ Meanwhile, trim and slice the aubergine into 1 cm (½ inch) rounds and spray each slice with low fat cooking spray. Grill for 3 to 4 minutes per side until tender. Cook the potatoes in a pan of boiling water for 5 minutes and then drain.

❹ Stir 3 tablespoons of the milk into the cornflour to form a paste. Heat the remaining milk until boiling and then pour over the cornflour. Stir well and return to the heat. Cook, stirring until the sauce thickens. Simmer for 2 minutes and then remove from the heat. Stir in the yogurt, nutmeg and Parmesan.

❺ Preheat the oven to Gas Mark 5/190°C/fan oven 170°C. Spoon the mince mixture into the base of an ovenproof dish. Top with the aubergine and potato slices and then pour the sauce over. Arrange the tomato slices over the top and bake for 40 minutes.

Grilled pork steaks with apple mash

Takes 45 minutes to prepare + 20 minutes marinating

| serves 4 | *POINTS* values per recipe 19 | calories per serving 350 | ❄ |

The apple in the mashed potatoes gives it a hint of sweetness that tastes wonderful with the pork.

4 x 125 g (4½ oz) boneless pork loin steaks
2 teaspoons clear honey
1 garlic clove, crushed
2 tablespoons soy sauce
1 tablespoon tomato purée
450 g (1 lb) potatoes, peeled and diced
225 g (8 oz) cooking apple, peeled, cored and diced
25 g (1 oz) low fat spread
6 spring onions, sliced
salt and freshly ground black pepper

❶ Score a criss cross pattern along the top of each pork steak and place them in a shallow dish. Mix together the honey, garlic, soy sauce and tomato purée and brush this mixture over the steaks. Cover and leave to marinate for 20 minutes.

❷ Meanwhile, cook the potatoes in lightly salted, boiling water for 15 minutes, and then add the apple to the pan. Cook for a further 5 minutes. Drain well and mash the apple and potatoes together. Season to taste.

❸ Grill the pork steaks under a medium to low heat for 5 minutes on each side.

❹ Melt the low fat spread in a small saucepan and add the spring onions. Cook for 2 minutes to soften them, and then spoon them into the mash and mix well.

❺ Divide the mash between four serving plates and top with a cooked pork steak.

Crêpes Suzette

Takes 30 minutes + 15 minutes standing

| serves 2 | *POINTS* values per recipe 7.5 | calories per serving 240 | ❄ | V |

This recipe doubles successfully for guests.

50 g (1¾ oz) plain flour
a pinch of salt
150 ml (5 fl oz) skimmed milk
1 egg
low fat cooking spray

FOR THE SAUCE
juice and zest of 1 orange
1 teaspoon caster sugar
15 g (½ oz) polyunsaturated margarine
1 tablespoon orange liqueur or brandy (optional)

❶ Sift the flour and salt into a bowl. Add half the milk and the egg and beat well until smooth. Stir in the rest of the milk and leave to stand for 15 minutes before cooking.

❷ Heat a small non stick frying pan and spray with the low fat cooking spray then ladle in enough pancake batter to just cover the base of the pan when you swirl it around.

❸ Fry until golden on the underside and then either flip, by tossing or with a palette knife or fish slice, and cook the other side. Slide out of the pan on to a plate and keep warm while you cook the rest of the crêpes.

❹ To make the sauce, heat the orange juice, zest and sugar in the frying pan, stirring, until the sugar is dissolved, then add the margarine and whisk. Fold the pancakes into quarters and add to the pan one by one turning in the sauce and then pushing to one side to fit the next in. Just before serving add the liqueur, if using, and ignite.

 **Pear brûlées**

Takes 15 minutes

serves **4**	**POINTS** values per recipe **9**	calories per serving **130**		**V**

These fruit brûlées are a low **POINTS** values version of this favourite dessert.

1 large ripe pear (e.g. Comice, Conference), chopped
200 g tub of Quark
140 g tub of flavoured low fat yogurt (e.g. lemon or vanilla)
4 tablespoons demerara sugar

❶ Preheat the grill. Divide the pear between four heatproof ramekins.

❷ Beat together the Quark and yogurt until smooth and spoon the mixture on top of the pears. Sprinkle the tops evenly with the sugar.

❸ Place the dishes under a very hot grill to caramelise the sugar until it dissolves. If you have a cook's blow torch you can flame the sugar with that.

❹ Cool the brûlées for 5 minutes before serving.

VARIATION All sorts of fruits could be used instead of pears. Try raspberries, sliced peaches, strawberries or plums, remembering to alter the **POINTS** values accordingly.

Crème caramel

Takes 15 minutes to prepare, 45 minutes to cook + 2 hours chilling

serves 6	*POINTS* values per recipe 15	calories per serving 186		V

Many people worry about making caramel, but if you follow the instructions you'll find that it's really very simple – it's just a case of having the patience to let the sugar dissolve completely, and then cooking it to the required toffee colour. Once you've mastered the technique, this classic French dessert is sure to become a firm favourite.

140 g (5 oz) granulated sugar
600 ml (1 pt) skimmed milk
4 eggs, beaten
1 teaspoon vanilla extract

❶ Preheat the oven to Gas Mark 2/150°C/fan oven 130°C.

❷ Place 110 g (4 oz) granulated sugar in a non stick pan with 4 tablespoons of boiling water and stir over a gentle heat until the sugar has completely dissolved.

❸ Increase the heat and boil the syrup until it reaches a rich golden brown colour, which will take around 5 minutes.

❹ Pour the caramel into a 20 cm (8 inch) diameter soufflé dish and swirl around to coat the base and sides of the dish. Leave to set.

❺ Add the milk and the remaining sugar to the caramel saucepan. Heat to simmering point, stirring to dissolve any caramel in the pan. Whisk the eggs and vanilla in a mixing bowl, and then gradually pour the hot milk over the eggs. Strain into the caramel coated soufflé dish through a sieve, to remove any egg threads.

❻ Place the dish in a roasting tin and fill the tin with hot water from the kettle. Bake in the oven for 45 minutes until the custard feels firm and set in the centre. Remove from

the hot water, leave to cool, then chill, covered, for at least 2 hours before serving.

❼ Run a palette knife around the edge of the dish and turn out on to a lipped dish to hold the sauce.

TOP TIP 1 Take care when making caramel, as boiling sugar can cause nasty burns. If there is any caramel left stuck to the pan, add hot water and bring to the boil to dissolve it.

TOP TIP 2 The crème caramel is cooked in a bath of hot water (known as a bain marie) to prevent the mixture from getting too hot and curdling. This method ensures a smooth, silky texture.

VARIATION You can make individual crème caramels in six 150 ml (¼ pint) ramekins.

(4) Queen of puddings

Takes 25 minutes to prepare + standing, 50 minutes to cook

serves 6	*POINTS* values per recipe **25.5**	calories per serving **270**		V

The different textured layers and oozing jam in this very traditional pudding make it hard to resist. Don't worry – it's still low in *POINTS* values!

600 ml (20 fl oz) semi skimmed milk
25 g (1 oz) low fat spread
grated zest of 1 lemon
4 large eggs, separated
100 g (3½ oz) caster sugar
150 g (5½ oz) fresh white breadcrumbs
low fat cooking spray
2½ tablespoons reduced sugar jam

❶ Preheat the oven to Gas Mark 4/180°C/fan oven 160°C.

❷ Warm the milk, low fat spread and lemon zest in a medium saucepan.

❸ Whisk in the egg yolks and 2 teaspoons of the caster sugar to make a custard.

❹ Place the breadcrumbs in a bowl and pour the custard over them. Mix thoroughly.

❺ Spray a 1.2 litre (2 pint) shallow ovenproof dish with low fat cooking spray. Pour the breadcrumb mixture into it and leave it to stand for 15 minutes.

❻ Bake in the oven for 25–30 minutes until just set – it should still be wobbly in the middle. Remove from the oven.

❼ Warm the jam and spread it over the pudding.

❽ Whisk the egg whites until stiff and then gradually add all the remaining sugar. Continue to whisk until you have a stiff and glossy meringue mixture.

❾ Pile the meringue mixture on top of the pudding and return it to the oven for 15–20 minutes, until the meringue is cooked and golden.

TOP TIP Always make sure the bowl you are whisking the egg whites in is completely free of grease or the whites will not whisk to a thick consistency.

VARIATION Try using other flavours of reduced sugar jam to make this pudding.

(3) French apple tart

Takes 25 minutes + 30 minutes chilling to prepare, 30 minutes to cook

| serves **6** | *POINTS* values per recipe **18** | calories per serving **205** | **V** |

This is a very simple way of making an apple tart. It looks pretty – and it tastes wonderful.

130 g (4¾ oz) plain white flour, plus 2 teaspoons for rolling
1 teaspoon fruit sugar (fructose)
65 g (2¼ oz) low fat spread
220 ml (7¼ fl oz) low fat custard, ready to serve
3 eating apples
1 teaspoon ground cinnamon
3 tablespoons reduced sugar apricot jam

❶ Preheat the oven to Gas Mark 6/ 200°C/fan oven 180°C.

❷ Place the flour and fruit sugar in a bowl. Add the low fat spread and with your fingertips, rub it into the dry ingredients until the mixture resembles fine breadcrumbs.

❸ Add approximately 2½ tablespoons of cold water to bind the pastry together. Wrap the pastry in clingfilm and leave it to rest in the fridge for 30 minutes.

❹ On a lightly floured surface, roll out the pastry and use it to line a 20 cm (8 inch) loose bottomed flan tin. Prick the surface with a fork and place the flan tin on a baking sheet. Bake in the oven for 15 minutes.

❺ Leave the pastry case to cool for 5 minutes then spoon in the custard.

❻ Peel, core and cut the apples into quarters and then into slices. Place the slices on top of the custard, arranging them so they are slightly overlapping, until the whole surface is covered.

❼ Sprinkle the apples with ground cinnamon.

❽ In a small saucepan, heat the apricot jam and then pour it over the apples. Return the tart to the oven for another 15 minutes. Serve hot or cold.

TOP TIP Leaving pastry to rest prevents it from shrinking while baking.

VARIATION A pear tart can be made in the same way. The *POINTS* values per serving will remain the same.

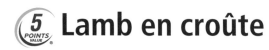 # Lamb en croûte

Takes 10 minutes to prepare, 25 minutes to cook

| serves **2** | *POINTS* values per recipe **9.5** | calories per serving **290** | ❄ |

175 g (6 oz) lamb loin fillet
3 spring onions, trimmed and sliced
1 small garlic clove, crushed
1 teaspoon soy sauce
15 g (½ oz) butter, melted
1 teaspoon wholegrain mustard
3 sheets of filo pastry
salt and freshly ground black pepper

❶ Preheat the oven to Gas Mark 6/200°C/fan oven 180°C.

❷ Make a horizontal slit through the lamb. Place the spring onions and garlic in a small pan with the soy sauce and cover. Heat gently for 1 minute until the spring onions wilt. Spoon into the slit in the lamb and then season well.

❸ Mix together the melted butter and mustard and use to brush over each sheet of filo pastry. Stack together and then use to wrap around the lamb fillet, tucking the edges under. Lift on to a non stick baking sheet and brush with any remaining butter and mustard mixture.

❹ Cook for 25 minutes and then serve carved into slices with freshly cooked vegetables.

 # Salmon and spinach parcels

Takes 20 minutes to prepare, 20 minutes to cook

| serves **4** | *POINTS* values per recipe **25** | calories per serving **385** |

If you are having friends around for dinner try this easy recipe. The crispy parcels look very impressive and taste delicious.

4 x 100 g (3½ oz) salmon fillets
150 g (5½ oz) baby spinach leaves
4 teaspoons low fat mayonnaise
8 sheets of filo pastry
25 g (1 oz) polyunsaturated margarine, melted
1 teaspoon poppy seeds
salt and freshly ground black pepper

❶ Preheat the oven to Gas Mark 5/190°C/fan oven 170°C. Rinse the salmon and pat it dry with kitchen paper.

❷ Place the spinach in a medium saucepan with 2 tablespoons of water and seasoning. Cover and simmer for 2–3 minutes, until the spinach wilts. Drain well.

❸ Place a quarter of the spinach over each salmon fillet and top each with a teaspoon of mayonnaise.

❹ Sandwich two sheets of filo pastry together with a light brushing of the melted margarine. Place a salmon fillet in the centre and wrap the pastry around it like a parcel. Repeat this process with the rest of the pastry and the remaining three salmon fillets. Brush the tops of the parcels with any remaining margarine and sprinkle with poppy seeds.

❺ Bake for 20 minutes, until the pastry is crisp and golden.

TOP TIP Because filo pastry is so thin it dries out very quickly and becomes brittle. To prevent this, keep the sheets of pastry covered with a damp tea towel until you are ready to use them.

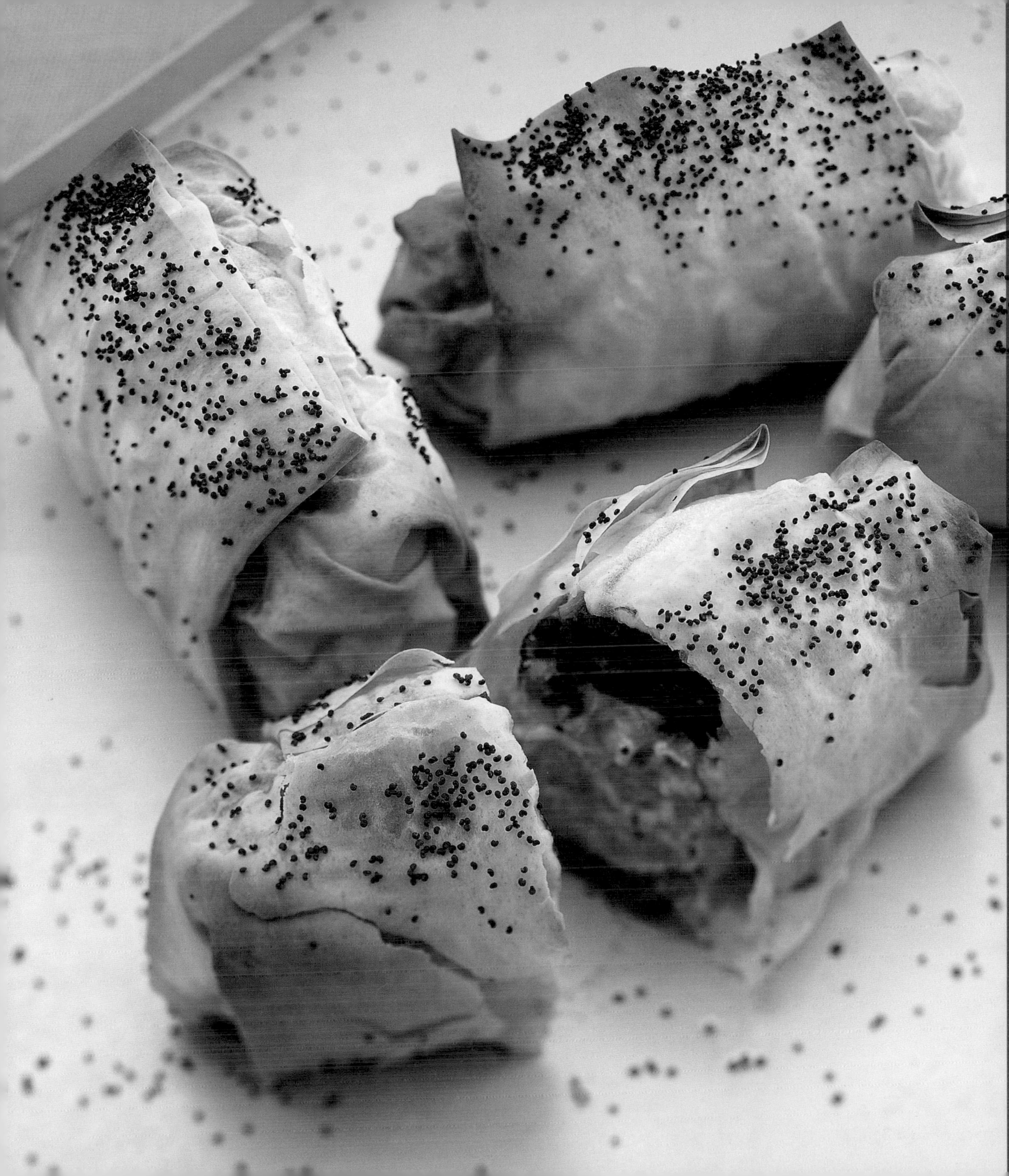

Special occasions

 # Sesame prawn toasts

Takes 35 minutes

makes **14**	**POINTS** values per recipe **14**	calories per serving **75**

A delicious low **POINTS** values version of this popular starter.

1 small (150 g/5½ oz) French stick, cut into 1 cm (½ inch) thick slices
80 g (3 oz) shelled prawns
80 g (3 oz) pork mince
1 spring onion, sliced finely
1 garlic clove, crushed
1 egg, beaten
½ teaspoon fish sauce (nam pla)
1 tablespoon chopped fresh coriander
2 tablespoons sesame seeds
2 tablespoons sweet chilli sauce
salt and freshly ground black pepper

❶ Toast the French stick slices on one side and set aside.

❷ Place the prawns in a blender and blend until nearly smooth. Add the pork and blend together with the prawns.

❸ Place the prawn and pork mixture in a bowl and add the other ingredients, apart from the sesame seeds and chilli sauce. Season and mix well.

❹ Heat a small frying pan and cook the prawn mixture for 3–4 minutes, stirring constantly.

❺ Preheat the grill and spoon the mixture on to the untoasted side of the bread. Press down well and then sprinkle with sesame seeds.

❻ Grill for 3–4 minutes, until the sesame seeds start to turn golden. Serve with chilli sauce.

TOP TIP When buying fresh coriander, choose deep green leaves – these will be the freshest and tastiest.

 **Spicy crab cakes**

Takes 30 minutes to prepare + 20 minutes chilling, 15 minutes to cook

serves **4**   *POINTS* values per recipe **4.5**   calories per serving **90**

These tasty crab cakes are perfect for a light lunch or served as a starter for a dinner party with friends. Serve with a green 0 *POINTS* value salad.

150 g (5½ oz) potatoes, peeled
250 g (9 oz) crabmeat
3 spring onions, sliced
½ teaspoon cayenne pepper
1 teaspoon wholegrain mustard
½ red pepper, de-seeded and chopped finely
grated zest and juice of ½ lime
1 tablespoon chopped fresh coriander
low fat cooking spray
salt and freshly ground black pepper

❶ Bring a small pan of salted water to the boil and add the potatoes. Cook for 8–10 minutes until tender. Drain and leave to cool.

❷ Place the remaining ingredients, except the low fat cooking spray, in a bowl.

❸ When the potatoes are cool enough to handle, grate them into the bowl.

❹ Mix well and shape into eight cakes. Place on a plate or tray and chill for 20 minutes.

❺ Heat a frying pan sprayed with low fat cooking spray and add the crab cakes. Cook for 3–4 minutes on each side.

(3 POINTS VALUE) Thai fish curry

Takes 25–30 minutes to prepare, 20–25 minutes to cook

serves **4**   *POINTS* values per recipe **12**   calories per serving **225**   ❄

Thousands of miles of coastline surround Thailand, so it's no surprise that fish curries are so popular there.

low fat cooking spray
6 shallots or 1 large onion, sliced
1 garlic clove, sliced thinly
200 ml (7 fl oz) reduced fat coconut milk
1 vegetable stock cube, dissolved in 425 ml (15 fl oz) boiling water
3–4 teaspoons Thai green curry paste
350 g (12 oz) butternut squash, peeled, de-seeded and cut into chunks
1 red pepper, de-seeded and cut into chunks
125 g (4½ oz) fine green beans, halved
2 tablespoons chopped fresh coriander
1 tablespoon Thai fish sauce or light soy sauce
1 teaspoon ready prepared 'fresh' ginger
1 teaspoon ready prepared 'fresh' lemongrass
1 fresh green chilli, de-seeded and sliced thinly (optional)
200 g (7 oz) haddock
200 g (7 oz) cooked large tiger prawns, with tails, defrosted if frozen
salt and freshly ground black pepper
sprigs of fresh coriander, to garnish

❶ Heat a large sauté pan or wok and lightly spray it with low fat cooking spray. Add the shallots or onion and garlic and cook over a medium heat for about 4–5 minutes, until softened.

❷ Add all the remaining ingredients, apart from the haddock, prawns and coriander. Bring to the boil. Reduce the heat and simmer gently for about 20–25 minutes, until the butternut squash is tender.

❸ Add the fish to the pan and cook for 2–3 minutes. Add the prawns and cook for another 2–3 minutes. Check the seasoning, adding salt and pepper, if needed.

❹ Ladle the curry into four bowls and serve, garnished with sprigs of fresh coriander.

TOP TIP Remember that curries have to be cooked according to your own taste, so it's better to add a little curry paste at first if you're not sure how hot you want it to be. You can always add a little more as you go.

VARIATION For a virtually vegetarian version, leave out the fish and prawns. Add extra 0 *POINTS* value vegetables, such as more peppers, courgettes and mushrooms. Make sure that you use soy sauce, not fish sauce. Remember that most varieties of Thai curry paste include dried shrimp in the ingredients. The *POINTS* values per serving will be 2.

Spinach and soft cheese roulade

Takes 35 minutes to prepare + 30 minutes cooling

serves **6**   *POINTS* values per recipe **12.5**   calories per serving **165**   **V**

Roulade mixtures are similar to those for soufflés and will puff up in the oven; as it cools, the roulade will shrink again, but this is quite normal.

200 g (7 oz) baby spinach leaves
a pinch of ground nutmeg
25 g (1 oz) polyunsaturated margarine
25 g (1 oz) plain white flour
200 ml (7 fl oz) skimmed milk
3 eggs, separated
125 g (4½ oz) low fat soft cheese with garlic and herbs
salt and freshly ground black pepper

❶ Place the spinach in a medium saucepan with the nutmeg and 2 tablespoons of water. Cover and cook for 2–3 minutes until the spinach has wilted. Drain, squeeze out any excess water and chop the spinach finely.

❷ Melt the margarine in a medium saucepan and stir in the flour. Gradually add the milk and cook, whisking until you have a thick, smooth sauce. Stir in the chopped spinach and seasoning, and then whisk in the egg yolks.

❸ Preheat the oven to Gas Mark 5/190°C/fan oven 170°C. Line a 23 cm x 28 cm (9 inch x 11 inch) Swiss roll tin with non stick baking parchment.

❹ Whisk the egg whites until they form soft peaks. Fold them into the spinach mixture and then turn it all into the prepared tin, and bake for 12 minutes.

❺ Turn the roulade out on to a clean sheet of non stick baking parchment and peel away the parchment lining the base. Roll up the roulade like a Swiss roll, using the clean sheet of baking parchment to guide it along. Allow it to cool for 30 minutes.

❻ Mash the soft cheese to soften it slightly. Carefully unroll the roulade and spread it with the soft cheese, and then re-roll. Serve cut into slices.

TOP TIP If you aren't keen on spinach, try using watercress instead. You will only need 150 g (5½ oz) watercress, with the tough stalks removed. The *POINTS* values will remain the same.

 # Mushroom pâté

Takes 10 minutes to prepare, 15 minutes to cook

| serves **4** | **POINTS** values per recipe **8** | calories per serving **120** | **V** |

This rich tasting mushroom pâté is served with melba toast and makes an elegant starter or lunchtime treat. A salad of mixed green leaves makes a good accompaniment.

250 g (9 oz) button mushrooms, ideally chestnut mushrooms
1 tablespoon low fat spread
1 large garlic clove, crushed
½ teaspoon dried thyme
1 tablespoon light soy sauce
200 g (7 oz) Quark
2 tablespoons finely chopped chives or green tops of spring onions
salt and freshly ground black pepper

FOR THE MELBA TOAST
4 medium slices of brown or white bread

❶ Set aside two mushrooms for a garnish and then finely chop the remainder. You can do this in a food processor.

❷ Melt the low fat spread in a large saucepan and lightly sauté the garlic for about 1 minute. Stir in the mushrooms, and then add 6 tablespoons of water, the thyme and seasoning.

❸ Heat the mixture until it starts sizzling. Cover the pan and cook gently for about 10–12 minutes, shaking the pan occasionally and stirring once or twice, quickly returning the cover to the pan. The mushrooms should soften in their own steam.

❹ Meanwhile, make the melba toast. Preheat the oven to Gas Mark 3/160°C/fan oven 140°C. Lightly toast the bread slices. Remove the crusts and then carefully cut through the soft centre of each toast to make two very thin slices. Now cut each thin slice diagonally to make four triangles and place them on a baking sheet. Bake them in the oven until the edges curl. Remove the toasts and cool them until crisp.

❺ Cool the mushrooms and stir in the soy sauce and Quark until you have a smooth and creamy mixture. Mix in the chives or spring onion tops. If you prefer a smooth pâté then purée everything in a food processor.

❻ Spoon the pâté mixture into a medium size bowl or divide it between four ramekin dishes. Slice the reserved mushrooms and arrange the slices on top. Chill in a refrigerator to make the texture firm.

2½ POINTS VALUE Teriyaki chicken salad

Takes 25 minutes + 30 minutes marinating

serves **4**   *POINTS* values per recipe **9.5**   calories per serving **185**

This tangy salad is an ideal starter for a dinner party – it will certainly wake up your tastebuds!

1 teaspoon groundnut oil
3 tablespoons soy sauce
1 garlic clove, crushed
2 tablespoons sherry
grated zest and segments of 1 orange
4 spring onions, sliced
3 x 165 g (5¾ oz) skinless chicken breasts, cut into strips
100 g (3½ oz) pak choi
50 g (1¾ oz) fresh beansprouts

❶ Mix together the groundnut oil, soy sauce, garlic, sherry, orange zest and the spring onions.

❷ Place the chicken in this marinade. Cover with clingfilm and place in the fridge for 30 minutes.

❸ Heat a griddle or wok and with a slotted spoon, transfer the chicken pieces to it. Reserve the marinade.

❹ Cook for 6–8 minutes, turning often, until the chicken is cooked through. Pour over the remaining marinade and cook for 1 or 2 minutes.

❺ Divide the pak choi, orange segments and beansprouts between four plates or shallow bowls and pour over the chicken pieces and juices. Serve.

TOP TIP Always make sure you heat the griddle or wok to a good temperature before you start cooking.

VARIATION For a more substantial meal, cook 60 g (2 oz) of egg noodles to serve with this dish. This will add an extra 3 *POINTS* values per serving.

(4) Chicken roulades

Takes 15 minutes to prepare, 25 minutes to cook

serves 2 **POINTS** values per recipe **8** calories per serving **245** ❄

2 x 175 g (6 oz) skinless chicken breasts
75 g (2¾ oz) low fat soft cheese
1 tablespoon finely chopped fresh chives
½ teaspoon Dijon mustard
1 teaspoon sun dried tomato purée
low fat cooking spray

❶ Preheat the oven to Gas Mark 4/180°C/fan oven 160°C. Line a baking tray with non stick baking parchment.

❷ Place each chicken breast between two pieces of greaseproof paper and, using the flat end of a rolling pin, hammer them out gently to about 1 cm (½ inch) thick. Peel away the greaseproof paper, and lay the breasts flat on a clean work surface.

❸ Beat together the soft cheese, chives, mustard and sun dried tomato purée, and spread equal amounts of this mixture over each chicken breast. Loosely roll up the breasts from the narrow end, enclosing the filling, and secure with one or two cocktail sticks.

❹ Place the chicken rolls on the baking tray and spray with low fat cooking spray. Bake them for 25 minutes.

❺ To serve, carefully remove the cocktail sticks. Slice each breast into rings. Arrange on warmed serving plates.

TOP TIP Hammer out the chicken breasts as evenly as possible without splitting the flesh.

(4½) Roast loin of pork with peaches and sage

Takes 20 minutes to prepare, 1 hour to cook

serves 6 **POINTS** values per recipe **28** calories per serving **435** ❄

Ideal for Sunday lunch. A fruity stuffing keeps the pork beautifully moist as it roasts. Serve with freshly cooked vegetables.

1 kg (2 lb 4 oz) boneless pork loin
1 teaspoon olive oil
2 shallots, chopped
4 canned peach halves in natural juice, chopped finely
1 teaspoon freeze dried sage
1 tablespoon flaked almonds
25 g (1 oz) fresh wholemeal breadcrumbs
1 tablespoon clear honey
salt and freshly ground black pepper

❶ Preheat the oven to Gas Mark 6/200°C/fan oven 180°C.

❷ Use a long bladed sharp knife to cut a slit right through the centre of the pork loin, forming a pocket for the filling.

❸ Heat the olive oil in a small pan and cook the shallots until softened. Remove from the heat and stir in the peaches, sage, almonds, breadcrumbs, honey and seasoning.

❹ Spoon into a piping bag fitted with a large plain nozzle and push the nozzle into the slit in the pork. Squeeze out the stuffing so that it fills the pocket.

❺ Lift into a non stick roasting tin. Season the top of the pork and roast for 1 hour. Leave to rest for 10 minutes before carving into slices.

Jungle curry

Takes 15 minutes to prepare, 15 minutes to cook

| serves **6** | **POINTS** values per recipe **10.5** | calories per serving **185** | ❄ | **V** |

A great curry with lots of crunchy vegetables – the perfect spicy vegetarian dish!

200 g (7 oz) long grain rice
low fat cooking spray
2 garlic cloves, crushed
2 cm (¾ inch) piece of fresh root ginger, peeled and chopped
1 lemon grass stick, chopped finely
1 teaspoon chilli flakes
1 teaspoon curry paste
1 large red onion, chopped
125 g (4½ oz) sugar snap peas
2 red peppers, de-seeded and chopped
100 g (3½ oz) baby corn, cut in half
2 courgettes, sliced
125 g (4½ oz) chestnut mushrooms
125 g (4½ oz) green beans
100 ml (3½ fl oz) vegetable stock
1 tablespoon soy sauce
150 g (5½ oz) fresh spinach

❶ Cook the rice according to the packet instructions.

❷ Heat a wok or large frying pan and spray with low fat cooking spray. Stir fry the garlic, ginger and lemon grass for 2–3 minutes before stirring in the chilli flakes and curry paste.

❸ Add the red onion, sugar snap peas, red peppers and baby corn and cook for 3–4 minutes, stirring constantly.

❹ Add the courgettes, chestnut mushrooms and green beans and then pour in the stock and soy sauce. Bring to the boil and continue to stir fry for a further 4–5 minutes.

❺ Finally, add the spinach and stir fry for a further 4–5 minutes until the spinach has wilted and the other vegetables are softening.

❻ Serve the curry in warmed bowls with the cooked rice.

TOP TIP Always cut away the outer leaves of lemon grass and only use the inner ones – the outer leaves are very tough.

Peppered sea bass with saffron mash

Takes 20 minutes to prepare, 25 minutes to cook

| serves **4** | **POINTS** values per recipe **24** | calories per serving **365** | ❄ |

4 x 150 g (5½ oz) sea bass steaks
1 tablespoon freshly ground mixed peppercorns
1 tablespoon chopped fresh parsley
1 teaspoon sunflower oil

FOR THE SAFFRON MASH
900 g (2 lb) potatoes, peeled and diced
8 saffron strands
1 tablespoon low fat spread
3 tablespoons low fat soft cheese
salt and freshly ground black pepper

❶ Bring a pan of lightly salted water to the boil and cook the potatoes until tender. While they are cooking, place the saffron in a small cup and add 2 tablespoons of boiling water. Leave to soak. Drain the cooked potatoes and mash with the saffron and liquid, low fat spread, soft cheese and seasoning.

❷ Meanwhile, rinse the fish and pat dry with absorbent kitchen paper. Mix together the ground mixed pepper and parsley and press on to one side of the sea bass.

❸ Wipe out a heavy based frying pan with the oil and heat until just smoking. Add the fish (peppered side up) to the pan and cook for 3 to 4 minutes. Turn over and cook for a further 1 to 2 minutes, until the fish is cooked through and has an opaque appearance. It really will depend on how thick the fish is as to how long it takes to cook but the flesh should flake easily when cooked.

❹ To serve, pile the saffron mash on to the centre of a warmed serving plate and top with a peppered sea bass portion.

TOP TIP Saffron is very expensive but a little goes a long way. It does have a flavour all of its own which goes so well with fish dishes. You can also get powdered saffron which is less expensive and can be used in this dish.

VARIATION If you prefer, you could use the same weight of cod fillets. The **POINTS** values will remain the same.

(6½ POINTS VALUE) Vegetable couscous with harissa

Takes 20 minutes to prepare, 30 minutes to cook

serves **4** · ***POINTS*** values per recipe **25.5** · calories per serving **560** · **V**

450 g (1 lb) quick cook couscous
low fat cooking spray
2 onions, quartered
225 g (8 oz) pumpkin, seeds removed, peeled and diced
225 g (8 oz) carrots, peeled and sliced
2 garlic cloves, crushed
a pinch of saffron strands
2 cinnamon sticks
2 tablespoons coriander seeds, crushed
1 teaspoon paprika
1 red chilli
225 g (8 oz) tomatoes
225 g (8 oz) courgettes
50 g (1¾ oz) raisins
175 g (6 oz) shelled fresh or frozen broad beans
450 ml (16 fl oz) vegetable stock
1 bunch of fresh coriander, chopped roughly, to garnish
sea salt and freshly ground pepper

FOR THE HARISSA
2 tablespoons tomato purée
1 garlic clove, crushed
1 teaspoon cayenne pepper
1 teaspoon ground coriander
1 teaspoon ground cumin
4 mint sprigs, chopped finely

❶ Put the couscous in a bowl and pour over enough boiling water to cover it plus 2.5 cm (1 inch). Cover the whole bowl with a plate or clingfilm and leave to steam.

❷ Spray a large pan with low fat cooking spray, then sauté the onions for 4 minutes, adding a tablespoon of water if they stick. Add the pumpkin, carrots and garlic and cook for another 3 minutes. Add the saffron, cinnamon, coriander, paprika and whole chilli. Lower the heat, cover and cook for 5 minutes.

❸ Meanwhile, chop the tomatoes into small dice and cut the courgettes into thick slices. Add to the pan with the raisins, broad beans and stock. Season and then cook uncovered for 20 minutes. Stir frequently until the vegetables are tender and the stock has been reduced and thickened.

❹ Make the harissa by mixing together all the ingredients, then add 4 tablespoons of the liquid from the stew.

❺ Remove the plate or clingfilm from the couscous and fluff up with a fork. Put on serving plates. Remove the cinnamon sticks from the stew and then spoon the stew over the couscous. Serve with the harissa and sprinkle with fresh coriander.

TOP TIP You could also buy the Bart Spice harissa mixture. The ***POINTS*** values per tablespoon will be 1.

(3) Frutti di bosco cheesecake

POINTS VALUE

Takes 15 minutes to prepare + cooling, 35 minutes to bake

serves 10	*POINTS* values per recipe 32	calories per serving 204	V

This rich and creamy cheesecake is baked in the oven to give a smooth texture. Frozen summer fruits are used for the 'frutti di bosco' (woodland fruits) topping, but you can also use fresh berries in season, or other tinned fruits such as peaches or mandarins, adjusting the *POINTS* values as needed.

110 g (4 oz) digestive biscuits, crushed
25 g (1 oz) Grape Nuts cereal
40 g (1½ oz) polyunsaturated margarine, melted
500 g (1 lb 2 oz) Quark
200 g (7 oz) very low fat plain fromage frais
60 g (2 oz) caster sugar
2 teaspoons vanilla extract
3 eggs
250 g (9 oz) frozen summer fruits, defrosted

❶ Preheat the oven to Gas Mark 4/180°C/fan oven 160°C.

❷ Mix the biscuit crumbs and cereal with the melted margarine then press into the base of a 20 cm (8 inch) spring form tin. Bake for 8 minutes until firm. Remove from the oven and reduce the temperature to Gas Mark 2/150°C/fan oven 130°C.

❸ Whisk the Quark, fromage frais, sugar, vanilla and eggs together until smooth. Pour on to the biscuit base and bake on the centre shelf for 35 minutes until the filling is set in the centre, but still slightly wobbly. Turn the oven off but leave the cheesecake in the oven as it cools down. This gradual temperature reduction stops the cheesecake from cracking as it cools.

❹ When at least 2 hours have passed, the cheesecake can be removed from the oven. Once at room temperature, cover and chill in the refrigerator.

❺ Take the cheesecake out of the fridge about 30 minutes before serving to take the chill off it. Carefully remove it from its tin, transfer to a plate and spoon the summer fruits on top. Serve, cut into slices.

TOP TIP The Grape Nuts cereal adds an extra crunch to the base, but you can leave it out if you prefer. The *POINTS* values per serving will remain the same.

 # Poached pears with hot chocolate sauce

Takes 15 minutes to prepare, 20 minutes to cook

| serves **4** | *POINTS* values per recipe **11.5** | calories per serving **135** | V |

4 pears, peeled
100 ml (3½fl oz) fresh orange juice
mint sprigs, to decorate (optional)

FOR THE SAUCE
2 single serve sachets of Options hot chocolate drink
200 g tub of low fat plain fromage frais
1 tablespoon clear honey

❶ Slice a thin piece from under each pear so they stand upright. Place in a small, deep saucepan and pour the orange juice and 300 ml (½ pint) water into the pan. Bring to the boil and reduce the heat. Cover and simmer for 20 minutes.

❷ Turn the heat off and allow the pears to cool in the cooking liquid.

❸ To make the sauce, empty the chocolate powder into a small jug and pour 50 ml (2 fl oz) boiling water over. Whisk well. Beat into the fromage frais with the honey.

❹ Serve the poached pears in a pool of chocolate sauce and decorate with a mint sprig, if desired.

VARIATION Low calorie hot chocolate drinks come in a variety of flavours. Chocolate orange or chocolate and hazelnut are excellent in this recipe.

 # Plum compote

Takes 5 minutes to prepare, 30 minutes to cook

| serves **4** | *POINTS* values per recipe **4** | calories per serving **95** | V |

This is a dish that is ideal for either the family or entertaining.

8 ripe but firm plums
150 ml (¼ pint) red wine
1 cinnamon stick
a few drops of vanilla extract
2 tablespoons soft brown sugar

❶ Preheat the oven to Gas Mark 4/180°C/fan oven 160°C.

❷ Put the plums in an ovenproof dish and pour the wine over them.

❸ Add the cinnamon stick and vanilla extract.

❹ Sprinkle the sugar on top and bake, uncovered, in the preheated oven for 30 minutes.

❺ Serve the plums with the flavoured wine spooned over them, discarding the cinnamon stick.

(4½ POINTS VALUE) Orange ginger treat

Takes 15 minutes

serves **4**	*POINTS* values per recipe **17.5**	calories per serving **190**		**V**

This luscious, layered dessert is perfect for a special occasion. It only takes a few minutes to put together and it tastes divine!

4 tablespoons whipping cream
125 g carton of diet orange yogurt
2 oranges, scrubbed
8 ginger thins
40 g (1½ oz) dark chocolate
mint or lemon balm leaves, to decorate

❶ Whip the cream in a chilled bowl until it holds its shape. Fold in the carton of yogurt. Chill for a few minutes.

❷ Meanwhile, use a zester to remove the zest from 1 orange. Reserve for decoration. Finely grate the zest from the other orange and fold through the cream mixture.

❸ Using a sharp serrated knife, remove all the peel and pith from the oranges, then cut them into segments, removing all the membrane.

❹ On separate serving plates, layer the biscuits with the cream mixture and orange segments.

❺ Melt the chocolate in a bowl placed over a saucepan of gently simmering water, then use to drizzle over the desserts. Decorate with the reserved orange zest and mint or lemon balm leaves.

TOP TIP You should serve these desserts shortly after you've made them; otherwise the biscuits will go soggy.

(3½ POINTS VALUE) Summer pavlova

Takes 25 minutes to prepare, 2½–3 hours to bake

serves **10**	*POINTS* values per recipe **36**	calories per serving **170**	❄	**V**

This spectacular creation is the perfect dessert for a summer celebration, although you can make it in winter with frozen berries if fresh ones are not available.

4 large egg whites
200 g (7 oz) caster sugar
200 ml (7 fl oz) whipping cream
225 g (8 oz) strawberries, sliced
225 g (8 oz) raspberries
strawberry leaves or mint leaves, to decorate

❶ Preheat the oven to Gas Mark 1/140°C/fan oven 120°C. Line a large baking sheet with non stick baking parchment and draw a 25 cm (10 inch) circle on it.

❷ In a large grease free bowl and using a hand held electric mixer, whisk the egg whites until they hold their shape. Gradually add the sugar, whisking well, until the egg whites are very stiff and glossy.

❸ Spread the meringue in an even layer over the marked out circle. Bake for 2½–3 hours. Remember that the meringue is dried out, rather than cooked, at this low temperature so an exact cooking time isn't necessary. It's a good idea to keep the oven door open just a fraction to get the best possible meringue.

❹ Remove the meringue from the oven. Cool it completely and then carefully peel away the baking parchment.

❺ When ready to serve, whip the cream until it holds its shape. Pile it on to the meringue and top with the strawberries and raspberries. Decorate with strawberry or mint leaves.

TOP TIP You can make the meringue base at least a week before you need it. It will store well, either in an airtight tin or wrapped in greaseproof paper.

VARIATION For a tropical fruit version, use 2 kiwi fruits, 1 mango and the juice and pulp from 2 passion fruit. The *POINTS* values per serving will remain the same.

Mango and raspberry stir fry with custard

Takes 15 minutes

| serves **2** | ***POINTS*** values per recipe **16** | calories per serving **330** | | **V** |

Serve warm (but not hot) to enjoy the flavours at their best.

15 g (½ oz) butter
1 ripe mango, peeled and sliced into strips
225 g (8 oz) fresh raspberries
200 ml (7 fl oz) reduced fat coconut milk
2 teaspoons cornflour
1 teaspoon caster sugar
grated zest and juice of ½ a lime

❶ Melt the butter in a large frying pan and fry the mango and raspberries for 2 minutes or until the juices begin to run. Using a slotted spoon, transfer to two shallow bowls.

❷ Heat all but 1 tablespoon of the coconut milk in the frying pan. Blend the remaining tablespoon with the cornflour, sugar and lime zest and juice. Stir this into the coconut milk in the frying pan and bring to the boil, stirring, until slightly thickened. (The sauce will take on a pinkish colour from the raspberries.)

❸ Serve warm, poured over the fruits.

TOP TIP If you wish to omit the coconut sauce, and enjoy the fruits on their own, you can save 3 ***POINTS*** values per serving.

VARIATIONS Bananas, pineapple, kiwi fruit and strawberries are all delicious cooked this way. Replace the raspberries with the equivalent weight of any of these fruits. Adjust the ***POINTS*** values accordingly.

(3) Tiramisu with strawberries

Takes 15 minutes + chilling

| serves **4** | **POINTS** values per recipe **12.5** | calories per serving **360** | **V** |

Tiramisu is the classic Italian favourite that literally means 'pick me up'. A restaurant version can easily clock up 10 **POINTS** values or more, so it's a great idea to make your own low **POINTS** values version.

150 ml (5 fl oz) strong coffee, cooled
2 tablespoons amaretto liqueur or Marsala
200 g tub of low fat soft cheese
200 ml (7 fl oz) very low fat plain fromage frais
1 teaspoon vanilla extract
powdered artificial sweetener, to taste
12 sponge fingers
2 teaspoons cocoa powder, for dusting
225 g (8 oz) strawberries, to serve

❶ In a shallow bowl, mix together the cooled coffee with the amaretto liqueur or Marsala.

❷ In another bowl, beat together the soft cheese, fromage frais and vanilla extract until smooth. Add a little sweetener to taste.

❸ Dip the sponge fingers briefly into the coffee mixture, layering half of them in the bases of four medium serving glasses or ramekin dishes. Top with half the cheese mixture. Repeat the layers. Cover the desserts and chill them in the fridge until you are ready to serve them.

❹ To serve, sprinkle each dessert with half a teaspoon of cocoa powder and serve with the strawberries.

(4½ POINTS VALUE) Banana and poppyseed tea bread

Takes 25 minutes to prepare, 1 hour to bake

| slices 8 | POINTS values per recipe 37 | calories per serving 290 | ❄ | V |

Fructose is a fruit sugar that is sweeter than sucrose – the sugar we generally use in cooking. Because fructose is sweeter we need to use less of it. It is generally available in all major supermarkets.

2 small bananas
2 tablespoons fresh lemon juice
100 g (3½ oz) polyunsaturated margarine
100 g (3½ oz) fructose
1/2 teaspoon grated nutmeg
1 tablespoon poppy seeds
2 eggs beaten
225 g (8 oz) self raising white flour
1 teaspoon baking powder

❶ Preheat the oven to Gas Mark 3/160°C/fan oven 140°C. Line a 700 g (1 lb 9 oz) loaf tin with non stick baking parchment.

❷ Peel the bananas and mash them thoroughly with the lemon juice, and set aside.

❸ Cream together the margarine and fructose until you have a pale and fluffy mixture. Add the nutmeg, poppy seeds, mashed bananas and beaten eggs.

❹ Sift the flour and baking powder into the mixture and fold it in thoroughly. Spoon it all into the prepared tin and level the top with the back of a metal spoon. Bake for 1 hour, or until a skewer inserted into the centre comes out clean.

TOP TIP Store in an airtight container for up to one week.

(2½ POINTS VALUE) Cumin shortbread

Takes 15 minutes + 10 minutes chilling time, 40 minutes to bake

| makes 8 | POINTS values per recipe 20 | calories per serving 145 | ❄ | V |

This light, spicy shortbread is ideal to serve after a light meal or with afternoon tea!

110 g (4 oz) low fat spread
50 g (1¾ oz) caster sugar
120 g (4¼ oz) plain flour
40 g (1½ oz) rice flour or cornflour
½ teaspoon ground cumin

❶ Preheat the oven to Gas Mark 4/180°C/fan oven 160°C.

❷ Beat the low fat spread in a bowl to soften.

❸ Add the sugar to the low fat spread and beat together. Sift in the flours and cumin and mix to a dough with a wooden spoon.

❹ Wrap the dough in clingfilm and chill for 10 minutes.

❺ Press the shortbread dough into a circle measuring approximately 20 cm (8 inches) on a baking sheet. Decorate the edges with a fork and gently mark out eight wedges with a knife.

❻ Bake for 40 minutes until golden. Remove from the oven and leave to cool slightly before placing on a cooling rack.

VARIATION For ginger shortbread, replace the ground cumin with ground ginger. The **POINTS** values will remain the same.

TOP TIP You can buy rice flour in health food shops.

(1½) Chocolate orange brownies

Takes 15 minutes to prepare, 20 minutes to bake

| serves **9** | *POINTS* values per recipe **14.5** | calories per serving **105** | ❄ | **V** |

Chocolate and orange are two ingredients that were just made for each other, and they taste wonderful in these delicious brownies.

low fat cooking spray
100 g (3½ oz) self raising white flour
4 tablespoons cocoa powder
1/2 teaspoon baking powder
1/4 teaspoon salt
2 egg whites
75 g (2¾ oz) light muscovado sugar
2 eggs, beaten
grated zest of 1 orange

❶ Preheat the oven to Gas Mark 5/190°C/fan oven 170°C. Spray an 18 cm (7 inch) square tin with low fat cooking spray.

❷ Sieve all the dry ingredients together into a bowl.

❸ In a grease free bowl, whisk the egg whites until they are stiff. Gradually add the sugar and whisk until the mixture is stiff and glossy.

❹ Beat the whole eggs and orange zest into the dry ingredients and, 1 tablespoon at a time, start gently folding in the egg white mixture.

❺ Spoon the mixture into the prepared tin and bake in the oven for 16–18 minutes.

❻ Leave the brownies to cool in the tin, and then turn out and cut them into nine squares.

② Apricot and cranberry squares

Takes 10 minutes to prepare, 17 minutes to bake

| makes **12** | **_POINTS_** values per recipe **24.5** | calories per serving **135** | ❄ | **V** |

These delicious fruity squares use a purée of apricots to make them moist and luscious. They taste wonderful served with a mug of steaming hot tea.

400 g can of apricots in juice, drained
250 g (9 oz) self raising white flour
1 teaspoon baking powder
1 teaspoon ground mixed spice or cinnamon
2 tablespoons sunflower oil
50 g (1¾ oz) dark soft brown sugar
4 tablespoons skimmed milk
1 large egg, beaten
3 tablespoons dried cranberries

❶ Preheat the oven to Gas Mark 5/190°C/fan oven 170°C. Line the base of a non stick Swiss roll tin with non stick baking parchment.

❷ Purée the apricots in a food processor.

❸ Put the flour, baking powder and spice into a large bowl and mix well with a wooden spoon.

❹ Add the oil, sugar, milk, egg and apricot purée and beat well. Stir in the cranberries.

❺ Spoon the mixture into the prepared tin. Level the surface and bake for about 17 minutes until the top feels springy.

❻ Cut the cake into 12 squares while still in the tin, and then turn out on to a wire rack and peel off the baking parchment.

TOP TIP These squares are perfect for the odd hungry moment. Spread them out on a wire tray and freeze solid. Tip into a plastic bag and store in the freezer. Thaw one at a time when needed!

VARIATION Use 400 g canned prunes in juice instead of the apricots. Be sure to stone them before putting them in the food processor. The **_POINTS_** values will remain the same.

(2) Chocolate scones

Takes 25 minutes

| makes **6** | **POINTS** values per recipe **12.5** | calories per serving **140** | ❄ | **V** |

Fresh baked scones hot from the oven are one of the nicest sweet treats – especially when they have a delicious chocolate flavour. The raspberry jam and creamy fromage frais filling will make them seem really indulgent, yet they are unbelievably low in **POINTS** values.

100 g (3½ oz) self raising white flour + 2 teaspoons for dusting
15 g (½ oz) cocoa powder
a good pinch of salt
½ teaspoon baking powder
1 tablespoon caster sugar
½ teaspoon vanilla extract
20 g (¾ oz) low fat spread
about 3–4 tablespoons skimmed milk
200 g tub of very low fat fromage frais
100 g (3½ oz) reduced sugar raspberry jam

❶ Heat the oven to Gas Mark 6/200°C/fan oven 180°C. Sift the flour, cocoa powder, salt and baking powder into a food processor. Add the sugar, vanilla extract and low fat spread and process until the mixture resembles fine breadcrumbs.

❷ Tip the mixture into a mixing bowl. Using a table knife, mix in the milk, adding spoonfuls until you have a firm but soft dough. You may not need all the milk and the dough should not be sticky.

❸ Turn out the dough on to a lightly floured board and knead it lightly until smooth. Pat it out to a 1.5 cm (⅝ inch) thickness and cut it into six 5 cm (2 inch) rounds, re-kneading any leftover dough.

❹ Place the rounds on a non stick baking tray or on a tray lined with non stick baking parchment. Bake for 12 minutes

until risen and the sides bounce back when pinched.

❺ Cool slightly and then halve them and fill with the fromage frais and jam. Top with more fromage frais and jam.

TOP TIP You don't have to cut scones in rounds. To save time, simply shape the dough into a round or square and cut it into six wedges or smaller squares.

(3) Easy cheesy scones

Takes 15 minutes to prepare, 15 minutes to bake

| makes **8** | ***POINTS*** values per recipe **25.5** | calories per serving **185** | ❄ | **V** |

Sometimes we crave a savoury rather than a sweet snack – these fit the bill perfectly.

225 g (8 oz) self raising white flour
1 teaspoon baking powder
a pinch of salt
1/2 teaspoon English mustard powder
50 g (1¾ oz) polyunsaturated margarine
75 g (2¾ oz) half fat Red Leicester cheese, grated
1 egg, beaten
150 ml (5 fl oz) skimmed milk

❶ Preheat the oven to Gas Mark 7/220°C/fan oven 200°C.

❷ Sift the flour and baking powder into a mixing bowl with the salt and mustard powder. Rub in the margarine, using your fingertips, until the mixture resembles fine breadcrumbs. Stir in the cheese and make a well in the centre.

❸ Beat together the egg and milk and pour this into the well. Mix together the dry and wet ingredients to form a soft dough. Shape the dough into a 20 cm (8 inch) circle and place it on a non stick baking tray.

❹ Mark eight wedges on the surface of the dough. Bake the scone for 15 minutes, until it is well risen and golden.

TOP TIP Try not to handle the dough too much, it doesn't require kneading as this will make the scones tough.

(1½) Ginger melting moments

Takes 15 minutes to prepare + cooling, 15 minutes to cook

| makes **16** | ***POINTS*** values per recipe **24** | calories per serving **90** | | **V** |

These classic biscuits are not just the easiest and quickest to make but possibly the easiest and quickest to eat!

low fat cooking spray
100 g (3½ oz) polyunsaturated margarine
40 g (1½ oz) icing sugar
1 tablespoon finely grated fresh root ginger or 1 teaspoon ground ginger
75 g (2¾ oz) self raising flour
75 g (2¾ oz) cornflour

❶ Preheat the oven to Gas Mark 5/190°C/fan oven 170°C and spray two baking sheets with low fat cooking spray.

❷ Cream the margarine and sugar together and then stir in the ginger and flours to make a stiff dough.

❸ Divide the dough into 16 pieces and roll into little balls. Place on the baking sheets, press down gently and bake for 15 minutes. Cool on the baking trays for a few minutes before transferring to a cooling rack.

TOP TIP These melting moments will keep for a week in an airtight container.

(1) Lemon and vanilla fingers

Takes 15 minutes to prepare, 10 minutes to bake

| makes **12** | ***POINTS*** values per recipe **12.5** | calories per serving **70** | **V** |

You'll find these delicious fingers very versatile. Simply nibble them on their own or serve them with fruit salads or iced desserts, remembering to add the extra ***POINTS*** values.

2 large eggs
85 g (3 oz) caster sugar
1 teaspoon vanilla extract
finely grated zest of 1 lemon
85 g (3 oz) plain white flour, sifted

❶ Grease and line a large, heavy metal baking sheet with non stick baking parchment. Heat the oven to Gas Mark 6/ 200°C/fan oven 180°C.

❷ Bring a medium size saucepan, half filled with water, to a gentle boil. Put the eggs, sugar and vanilla extract into a large heatproof bowl and place the bowl over the pan of water. Using an electric hand held whisk (or balloon whisk if you have to beat by hand) beat as fast as possible until you have a firm, pale golden foam – the mixture should leave a trail when you lift out the beaters.

❸ Remove the bowl from the heat and continue whisking for 2–3 minutes and then gently fold in the lemon zest and flour using a large metal spoon.

❹ Fit a plain 1.5 cm (⅝ inch) nozzle into a piping bag. Put the bag into a tall jug and roll down the top. Spoon the mixture into the piping bag.

❺ Twist the top to seal the bag with one hand and holding the nozzle in the other hand, pipe 12 straight lengths about 10 cm (4 inches) long on to the baking sheet. If you don't own a piping bag, spoon mounds of the mixture, flattening them with the back of a teaspoon to make 12 rounds about 3 cm (1¼ inches) in diameter.

❻ Bake for 5–7 minutes until the biscuits are pale golden and firm. Cool for 2 minutes, and then lift the fingers off the baking sheet with a palette knife on to a wire tray. Let them cool completely.

TOP TIP Eggs used for baking should be at room temperature. That way they whisk to a better volume. If you store eggs in the fridge, remove them 30 minutes before use.

(2½ POINTS VALUE) Chocolate chip cookies

Takes 10 minutes to prepare, 15 minutes to cook

| makes **16** | **POINTS** values per recipe **41** | calories per serving **150** | ❄ | **V** |

These American style chocolate chip cookies are ideal for when you feel you want something sweet to nibble. They're so good, you'll want to make room for them in your Weight Watchers Programme.

low fat cooking spray
110 g (4 oz) polyunsaturated margarine
110 g (4 oz) light muscovado sugar
1 egg, beaten
150 g (5½ oz) plain white flour
a pinch of salt
½ teaspoon baking powder
75 g (2¾ oz) rolled oats
50 g (1¾ oz) plain chocolate drops

❶ Preheat the oven to Gas Mark 4/180°C/fan oven 160°C. Spray two baking sheets with low fat cooking spray.

❷ Beat the margarine and sugar together in a mixing bowl until it has a light, fluffy texture and is much paler in colour. Beat in the egg, a little at a time.

❸ Sift in the flour, salt and baking powder. Add the rolled oats and half the chocolate drops. Stir all the ingredients together until the mixture is combined.

❹ Using a tablespoon, place eight heaps of the mixture on to each baking sheet, allowing room for them to spread. Transfer to the oven and bake for 12–15 minutes, until golden.

❺ When you take the cookies out of the oven, sprinkle them with the remaining chocolate drops. After a few minutes, transfer the cookies to a wire rack to cool completely.

VARIATION Use 25 g (1 oz) of chopped hazelnuts instead of the 50 g (1¾ oz) of chocolate drops – the **POINTS** values per cookie will be 2½. You can use 15 g (½ oz) of both nuts and chocolate drops if you like. The **POINTS** values will be 2½ per cookie.

Orange and sesame flapjacks

Takes 15 minutes to prepare, 20 minutes to cook

| serves **8** | ***POINTS*** values per recipe **54.5** | calories per serving **330** | | **V** |

125 g (4¾ oz) butter
125 g (4¾ oz) demerara sugar
3 tablespoons golden syrup
finely grated zest of 1 orange
2 tablespoons sesame seeds
1 teaspoon ground cinnamon
225 g (8 oz) rolled oats

❶ Preheat the oven to Gas Mark 5/190°C/fan oven 170°C. Line an 8-inch (20 cm) square cake tin with non stick baking parchment.

❷ Place the butter, sugar and syrup in a small saucepan and heat gently until dissolved.

❸ Mix together the orange zest, sesame seeds, cinnamon and oats. Pour the melted butter mixture over and stir well. Press into the lined tin.

❹ Bake for 20 minutes. Allow to cook for 5 minutes. Mark into eight squares. Allow to cool.

 # Yorkshire curd tarts

Takes 20 minutes to prepare, 20 minutes to bake

| makes **12** | ***POINTS*** values per recipe **24** | calories per serving **115** | ❄ | **V** |

These melt in the mouth treats are rather like mini cheesecakes, but are much lower in ***POINTS*** values!

175 g (6 oz) ready made shortcrust pastry, defrosted if frozen
125 g (4½ oz) low fat cottage cheese
finely grated zest of 1 lemon
25 g (1 oz) sultanas
25 g (1 oz) demerara sugar
a pinch of ground nutmeg
1 egg

❶ Preheat the oven to Gas Mark 5/190°C/fan oven 170°C. Roll out the pastry and cut out circles. Fit them in a 12 hole patty tin.

❷ Push the cottage cheese through a sieve and beat it well with the lemon zest, sultanas, sugar, nutmeg and egg.

❸ Divide the filling between the pastry cases and bake for 20 minutes, until the filling is just set to the touch.

TOP TIP As a change, try adding grated orange zest instead of lemon and using ground cinnamon instead of the nutmeg. Dust 1 teaspoon of icing sugar over the total number of tarts, if desired, which will not alter the ***POINTS*** values.

$2\frac{1}{2}$ POINTS VALUE Carrot cup cakes

Takes 15 minutes to prepare, 15 minutes to bake

makes **9**   *POINTS* values per recipe **21**   calories per serving **145**   V

Carrot cake is one of the great delicious cake mixtures of all time. Grated carrot and ripe bananas add moistness, which enables you to cut down on *POINTS* values without losing any of the flavour.

100 g (3½ oz) self raising white flour
1 teaspoon baking powder
½ teaspoon ground cinnamon
50 g (1¾ oz) polyunsaturated margarine
100 g (3½ oz) soft brown sugar
1 teaspoon vanilla extract
1 egg
2 tablespoons skimmed milk
1 small ripe banana, chopped roughly
1 carrot, grated coarsely
1 teaspoon icing sugar, for dusting

❶ Preheat the oven to Gas Mark 5/190°C/fan oven 170°C. Line a bun tin with nine paper baking cases.

❷ Put the flour, baking powder, cinnamon, margarine, sugar, vanilla extract, egg, milk and banana in a food processor and blend until smooth, scraping down the sides once or twice.

❸ Mix in the carrot, blending it in with short pulses of the food processor until just incorporated.

❹ Spoon the mixture into the paper cases and bake for about 15–17 minutes until firm and springy on top.

❺ Place the cakes on a wire rack and dust the tops with icing sugar.

Sponge cake with summer berries

Takes 30 minutes

| serves **6** | **POINTS** values per recipe **18** | calories per serving **190** | ❄ | **V** |

low fat cooking spray

3 large eggs

100 g (3½ oz) golden caster sugar

100 g (3½ oz) plain white flour, sifted

2 tablespoons reduced sugar strawberry jam

50 g (1¾ oz) fresh strawberries, halved

50 g (1¾ oz) fresh raspberries

50 g (1¾ oz) blackcurrants or blueberries

TO DECORATE

mint leaves (optional)

½ teaspoon icing sugar

❶ Preheat the oven to Gas Mark 7/220°C/fan oven 200°C. Spray two 18 cm (7 inch) sandwich tins with the cooking spray and line the bases with circles of greaseproof paper.

❷ In a large, clean bowl whisk the eggs and the sugar together until very pale and light in texture; this will take about 5 minutes with an electric beater. You'll know when the mixture is thick enough if you lift the beaters and they leave a trail for a few seconds.

❸ Using a metal spoon, fold the flour into the mixture carefully but thoroughly. Divide the mixture between the prepared tins, and level the surface.

❹ Bake for 8–10 minutes until golden brown and springy to the touch. Remove from the oven and turn out on to a cooling rack. Remove the greaseproof paper. Cover with a clean damp tea towel and leave until completely cold.

❺ Spread the strawberry jam on the surface of one sponge and scatter most of the fruit over it. Top with the second sponge and decorate with the remaining fruit and the mint leaves, if using. Finish with sprinkled icing sugar.

⓵ Baked doughnuts

Takes 15 minutes

| makes **6** | ***POINTS*** values per recipe **12.5** | calories per serving **70** | ❄ | **V** |

You can buy special doughnut trays from empirestores, online or by phone, for baking these doughnuts. It's definitely worth trying the recipe, as the doughnuts make a delicious treat.

100 g (3½ oz) plain flour
1 teaspoon baking powder
1 egg, beaten
1 teaspoon corn oil
½ teaspoon vanilla extract
75 g (2¾ oz) caster sugar
4 tablespoons skimmed milk
½ teaspoon salt
low fat cooking spray

TO SERVE
4 teaspoons caster sugar
½ teaspoon ground cinnamon

❶ Preheat the oven to Gas Mark 3/160°C/fan oven 140°C.

❷ Combine all the ingredients to form a smooth batter.

❸ Spray the baking tray with low fat cooking spray. Almost fill each doughnut hole, making sure you do not over fill (or, when cooked, the doughnuts will have no holes!)

❹ Cook for 8–10 minutes, until risen and firm to the touch.

❺ On a small plate, mix together the sugar and cinnamon for serving.

❻ Remove the cooked doughnuts from the tin. Dip the bottom of each in the sugar and cinnamon mix and leave to cool on a rack.

Eazi freeze lemon sponge

Takes 15 minutes to prepare, 1 hour to cook

serves 16	*POINTS* values per recipe 50.5	calories per serving 190	❄	V

If you wrap and freeze pieces individually, you'll have the ideal solution for perfect portion control. This is delicious with 2 tablespoons of virtually fat free fromage frais. The *POINTS* values per recipe will remain the same.

low fat cooking spray
juice and finely grated zest of 1 lemon
150 g (5½ oz) caster sugar
150 ml carton low fat plain yogurt
150 ml (5 fl oz) sunflower oil
250 g (9 oz) self raising flour
2 large eggs

❶ Preheat the oven to Gas Mark 3/160°C/fan oven 140°C. Spray a 20 cm (8 inch) round cake tin with low fat cooking spray and line with greaseproof paper.

❷ Put the lemon juice into a bowl and add one teaspoon of the caster sugar.

❸ Put the lemon zest into a large mixing bowl and add the remaining sugar, yogurt, oil, flour, and eggs. Beat together for 1 minute with a wooden spoon to mix thoroughly.

❹ Pour the mixture into the prepared tin, then transfer to the middle shelf of the oven and bake for approximately 1 hour or until risen and springy when lightly touched.

❺ Stand the cake tin on a cooling rack, and while hot, slowly spoon the lemon juice mixture over the cake. Allow to cool in the tin.

❻ When complete cooled, cut the cake into 16 portions.

TOP TIP 1 Wrap the portions not required in freezer wrap, then freeze for up to 2 months. Only defrost portions required, to reduce temptation.

TOP TIP 2 Use the empty yoghurt carton as an easy measure to make the cake even quicker to prepare. You'll need 2 x caster sugar, 1 x sunflower oil and 3 x self raising flour. The *POINTS* values per recipe remain the same.

VARIATION Try using orange zest and juice for a change.

(3) Devil's food cake

Takes 25 minutes to prepare, 20 minutes to cook

| serves **10** | **POINTS** values per recipe **30.5** | calories per serving **197** | ❄* | **V** |

*Freezing recommended for sponge only

Deliciously moist and dense, it's hard to believe that such an intensely chocolatey cake could be so low in **POINTS** values, but it really is true. This is a perfect birthday or celebration cake for a chocoholic!

40 g (1½ oz) polyunsaturated margarine
100 g (3½ oz) light brown soft sugar
1 teaspoon vanilla extract
3 egg whites
5 tablespoons low fat plain yogurt
150 g (5½ oz) self raising flour
25 g (1 oz) cocoa powder
½ teaspoon baking powder
½ teaspoon bicarbonate of soda
150 ml (5 fl oz) skimmed milk
25 g (1 oz) finely grated dark chocolate
25 g (1 oz) caster sugar
salt

FOR THE ICING
200 g extra light cream cheese
3 tablespoons granulated sweetener
2 tablespoons cocoa powder, sifted

❶ Preheat the oven to Gas Mark 4/180°C/fan oven 160°C, and grease and line 2 x 18 cm (7 inch) cake tins with baking paper.

❷ Beat the margarine, sugar, vanilla extract and 1 egg white together for 2 minutes using an electric whisk, until pale and smooth. Gradually beat in the yogurt.

❸ Sift the flour, cocoa powder, baking powder, bicarbonate of soda and a pinch of salt together. Add a third of these dry ingredients to the wet, followed by half the milk. Beat until smooth, then whisk in the remaining flour mixture and milk. Fold in two thirds of the grated chocolate.

❹ Clean the beaters then whisk the remaining 2 egg whites to soft peaks in another bowl. Whisk in the caster sugar until shiny. Using a large metal spoon, stir a spoonful of egg whites into the cake batter to loosen it and then carefully fold in the remainder.

❺ Divide the batter between the prepared tins and bake on the centre shelf for 18–20 minutes, or until risen and springy in the centre. Turn out on to a wire rack to cool.

❻ To make the icing, simply beat the icing ingredients together until smooth. Sandwich the cakes together with a third of the icing then spread the remainder over the top and sides. Scatter over the reserved grated chocolate.

TOP TIP Use a really good quality dark chocolate with at least 50% cocoa solids (check the ingredients panel) rather than ordinary cooking chocolate, to give this cake its depth of flavour.

Marbled vanilla and coffee cake

Takes 20 minutes to prepare, 35 minutes to bake

| makes **12** | *POINTS* values per recipe **34.5** | calories per serving **170** | ❄ | **V** |

This is great fun to make. The best part is slicing into the cake and seeing the marbled patterns!

100 g (3½ oz) polyunsaturated margarine
100 g (3½ oz) caster sugar
2 eggs
175 g (6 oz) self raising white flour
3 tablespoons skimmed milk
1 teaspoon vanilla essence
3 tablespoons strong black coffee

FOR THE TOPPING
100 g (3½ oz) low fat soft cheese
1 teaspoon strong black coffee
2 tablespoons granulated artificial sweetener

❶ Preheat the oven to Gas Mark 5/190°C/fan oven 170°C. Line a 20 cm (8 inch) round cake tin with non stick baking parchment.

❷ Cream together the margarine and sugar until the mixture is pale and fluffy. Add the eggs and beat well. Sift the flour into the mixture and fold it in thoroughly using a metal spoon.

❸ Divide the mixture between two bowls. Mix the skimmed milk and vanilla essence into one bowl, and the coffee into the other.

❹ Drop alternating spoonfuls of the mixture into the prepared tin, dragging a skewer through the mixtures to blend them into each other. Bake for 30–35 minutes, until the cake is well risen and springy to the touch.

❺ Carefully remove the cake from the tin and allow it to cool completely on a wire rack.

❻ To decorate, beat the soft cheese with the coffee and sweetener and spread it over the surface, using a fork to mark a pattern on the top.

(3½ POINTS VALUE) Spicy nuts

Takes 5 minutes to prepare, 15 minutes to cook

| serves **8** | *POINTS* values per recipe **27.5** | calories per serving **205** | | **V** |

Delicious to nibble with a pre dinner drink and much more impressive than opening a packet!

1 teaspoon salt
¼ teaspoon artificial sweetener
½ teaspoon ground ginger
½ teaspoon ground coriander
½ teaspoon ground cinnamon
½ teaspoon ground cumin
½ teaspoon garam masala
100 g (3½ oz) cashew nuts
100 g (3½ oz) pecan nuts
50 g (1¾ oz) almonds
low fat cooking spray

❶ Preheat the oven to Gas Mark 6/200°C/fan oven 180°C.

❷ Mix together the salt, sweetener and all the spices. Add 1 tablespoon of water to make a paste.

❸ Mix the nuts together in a bowl and add the paste. Mix really well to coat the nuts in the paste.

❹ Spray a roasting tray with low fat cooking spray and pour in the nuts.

❺ Cook in the oven for 10 minutes. Stir the nuts and then cook for a further 5 minutes. Remove from the oven and allow to cool in the tin.

TOP TIP These nuts will keep for a few days if stored in an airtight container.

VARIATION Any combination of nuts work well in this recipe – try peanuts and Brazil nuts instead of the cashew and pecan nuts. The *POINTS* values per serving will remain the same.

① Tasty topped blinis

Takes 10 minutes

| makes **16** | **POINTS** values per recipe **9.5** | calories per serving **35** |

Nibbles and party food have to be quick to make and definitely hassle-free, otherwise the whole purpose of entertaining friends becomes stressful and a chore. Even strong wills can weaken at times like this! So try these little low **POINTS** values pancakes, crowned with tasty toppings.

135 g pack of blinis (Russian style pancakes)

FOR THE SMOKED SALMON AND HORSERADISH TOPPING
1 tablespoon horseradish relish
1 tablespoon 0% fat Greek style yogurt
1 small cooked beetroot, chopped
75 g (2¾ oz) smoked salmon trimmings
freshly ground black pepper
snipped fresh chives, to garnish

FOR THE TURKEY AND TOMATO TOPPING
2 tablespoons half fat crème fraîche
1 tablespoon tomato or onion relish
3–4 wafer thin slices smoked turkey, cut into pieces
flat leaf parsley, to garnish

❶ Warm the blinis through under a low grill setting, just to refresh them.

❷ To assemble the smoked salmon blinis, mix together the horseradish and yogurt. Spread a little over each blini, top with some beetroot and finally a folded piece of salmon. Garnish with the snipped chives and pepper.

❸ To make the turkey blinis, spoon some cremè fraîche on to each blini, then a dollop of relish followed by the turkey. Garnish with a tiny sprig of parsley.

❹ Serve allowing one of each per portion.

TOP TIP Blinis are little Russian style pancakes and are available at supermarkets ready made. You can also use little toasts or slices of baguette as an alternative. Or use a small pitta bread, split in half then cut into 10 pieces and baked until crisp.

VARIATION Relishes and pickle tend to be quite low fat, so experiment with different flavours.

(1) Baby potato bites

POINTS VALUE

Takes 15 minutes to prepare, 30–40 minutes to cook

| makes **16** | **POINTS** values per recipe **16** | calories per serving **35*** |

*35 calories per potato half with all toppings except crème fraîche and chilli topping, which is 30

8 small potatoes (e.g. Charlotte)
2 tablespoons olive oil
coarse ground salt and black pepper

FOR THE CORONATION CHICKEN TOPPING
25 g (1 oz) cooked chicken, chopped
1 tablespoon chopped red pepper
2 tablespoons virtually fat free fromage frais
1 teaspoon curry paste
1 teaspoon mango chutney
chopped fresh parsley, to garnish

FOR THE CRÈME FRAÎCHE AND CHILLI TOPPING
2 tablespoons half fat crème fraîche
1 teaspoon finely chopped green chilli
1 spring onion, chopped finely

FOR THE PRAWN AND TOMATO SALSA TOPPING
2 tablespoons 95% fat free fresh tomato salsa
8 cooked prawns
4 tiny sprigs of fresh coriander

❶ Preheat the oven to Gas Mark 5/190°C/fan oven 170°C. Toss eight small potatoes in the oil and tip into a shallow roasting pan. Sprinkle with salt and pepper and roast for 30–40 minutes until tender. Leave until cool enough to handle.

❷ Meanwhile make up the toppings – each is sufficient for four potato halves. Simply combine the ingredients together for each option, leaving some chopped herbs to garnish.

❸ Cut the potatoes in half and then top the warm potatoes with your choice of topping(s). Arrange on a plate and serve immediately.

TOP TIP The potatoes can be cooked up to 2 hours ahead. Do not cut them in half until needed. Cool, cover and keep in the refrigerator. Either warm up before serving or serve them at room temperature.

VARIATION Try a blue cheese and chive topping for 1½ **POINTS** values per potato half. Mix together 25 g (1 oz) blue cheese, 1 tablespoon half fat crème fraîche and 1 teaspoon chopped chives.

Hot cross buns

Takes 25 minutes to prepare, 20 minutes to bake + 1½ hours rising

| makes **16** | ***POINTS*** values per recipe **33.5** | calories per serving **135** | ❄ | **V** |

350 g (12 oz) strong white flour, plus 2 tablespoons for kneading

100 g (3½ oz) granary flour

15 g (½ oz) easy blend yeast

1 teaspoon caster sugar

½ teaspoon salt

1 teaspoon ground mixed spice

50 g (1¾ oz) currants

50 g (1¾ oz) chopped mixed peel

150 ml (5 fl oz) hand hot skimmed milk

25 g (1 oz) polyunsaturated margarine, melted

low fat cooking spray

1 tablespoon clear honey, warmed

❶ Sift the strong white flour into a mixing bowl. Stir in the granary flour, easy blend yeast, sugar, salt, mixed spice, currants and mixed peel.

❷ Mix together 150 ml (5 fl oz) hand hot water, milk and melted margarine and pour this over the dry ingredients. Using clean hands, mix thoroughly until you have a soft dough.

❸ Turn out the dough on to a clean work surface and, using a little of the extra flour to prevent sticking, knead the dough for 5 minutes.

❹ Lightly spray a large bowl with low fat cooking spray – this will prevent the dough from sticking. Place the dough in the bowl and cover with a damp tea towel. Leave the dough to rise in a warm place for 1 hour.

❺ Turn the dough out on to a lightly floured surface and knead again for 2–3 minutes. Divide the dough into 16 pieces and shape them into balls.

❻ Arrange the dough balls on two non stick baking trays and, using a sharp knife, mark a cross on the top of each one. Cover both trays with a damp tea towel again and leave in a warm place for 30 minutes, until the buns have risen. Preheat the oven to Gas Mark 6/200°C/fan oven 180°C.

❼ Bake the buns for 15–20 minutes, until they are golden. To test if they are cooked, tap the base of the buns – they should sound hollow.

❽ Transfer the buns to a cooling rack and brush the tops with a little warmed honey while they are still hot.

Pancakes with lemon, lime and liqueur

Takes 10 minutes to prepare, 15 minutes to cook

| serves **4** | ***POINTS*** values per recipe **14.5** | calories per serving **195** | **V** |

Whisk up this easy all in one batter to make pancakes. It's the perfect recipe for Shrove Tuesday, especially when flavoured with a little liqueur or brandy.

100 g (3½ oz) plain flour
a pinch of salt
1 egg
300 ml (½ pint) skimmed milk
finely grated zest and juice of 1 lime
finely grated zest and juice of 1 lemon
2 teaspoons vegetable oil
1 tablespoon caster sugar
2 tablespoons Cointreau, Grand Marnier or brandy

❶ Sift the flour and salt into a large bowl. Add the egg, milk and grated lime and lemon zest and whisk together until smooth. Alternatively, put the ingredients into a liquidiser or food processor and blend for 15–20 seconds until smooth.

❷ Heat a small, heavy based, frying pan. Add a few drops of oil and pour in some batter, tilting the pan so that the mixture spreads over the base to make a thin pancake.

❸ When the pancake has set on the surface, flip it over to cook the other side. Make eight pancakes in this way, transferring them to kitchen paper as you cook them. When all the pancakes are cooked, fold them into triangles.

❹ Wipe the frying pan with a piece of kitchen paper, then add the lime and lemon juice and sugar. Heat gently to dissolve, then add the liqueur or brandy.

❺ Return all the pancakes to the frying pan, overlapping them to fit. Cook gently for about 1 minute to re-heat. Serve two pancakes per person.

(3½ POINTS VALUE) Carrot and orange Easter cake

Takes 20 minutes to prepare, 1½ hours to cook

| serves 12 | *POINTS* values per recipe 42 | calories per serving 220 | ❄ | V |

This delicious carrot cake is perfect for Easter! To decorate, choose some pretty spring flowers, such as primroses, violets or tiny rosebuds and brush their petals with lightly beaten egg white. Dip into caster sugar, then leave to dry on sheets of greaseproof paper.

low fat cooking spray
100 g (3½ oz) polyunsaturated margarine
100 g (3½ oz) light muscovado sugar
3 eggs, beaten
175 g (6 oz) carrots, grated finely
225 g (8 oz) self raising flour
a pinch of salt
1 teaspoon baking powder
1 teaspoon ground mixed spice
2 teaspoons finely grated orange zest
40 g (1½ oz) sultanas or raisins

FOR THE TOPPING
175 g (6 oz) low fat soft cheese
1 tablespoon icing sugar

TO DECORATE
orange zest
lemon zest

❶ Preheat the oven to Gas Mark 4/180°C/fan oven 160°C. Spray a 20 cm (8 inch) round cake tin with low fat cooking spray and line with greaseproof paper.

❷ Warm the margarine and sugar together over a low heat, until the sugar has dissolved. Cool slightly.

❸ In a large bowl, combine the eggs, carrots and melted butter and sugar. Sift in the flour, salt, baking powder and mixed spice. Add the orange zest and sultanas or raisins and mix well.

❹ Transfer to the prepared tin, level the surface and bake for about 1 hour 10 minutes, until firm to the touch. Check with a fine skewer; it should come out clean. Cool for 10 minutes, then turn out and cool completely on a wire rack.

❺ To decorate, beat the soft cheese and icing sugar together. Spread over the cake and sprinkle with orange and lemon zest.

TOP TIP This cake can be kept in the refrigerator for 2–3 days.

(6) Chocolate nests

Takes 15 minutes + 20 minutes chilling

| makes **8** | ***POINTS*** values per recipe **47.5** | calories per serving **190** | ❄ | **V** |

The perfect recipe for Easter.

125 g (4½ oz) dark chocolate
40 g (1½ oz) polyunsaturated margarine
3 Shredded Wheat biscuits
24 mini chocolate eggs

❶ Melt the chocolate and margarine together by putting them into a large heatproof bowl placed over a saucepan of gently simmering water. When smooth and melted, remove from the heat.

❷ Break up the Shredded Wheat biscuits and stir into the chocolate mixture.

❸ Spoon the mixture into paper bun cases, making slight depressions in the centre of each one to form a nest. Chill in the refrigerator until firm, about 20 minutes.

❹ Serve with 3 tiny chocolate eggs in each nest.

TOP TIP You can reduce the ***POINTS*** values by having just 1 mini chocolate egg.

(4) Roast turkey with Madeira sauce

Takes 20 minutes to prepare + 1¼–1½ hours to cook

| serves **4** | **POINTS** values per recipe **15.5** | calories per serving **255** | ❄ |

800 g (1 lb 11 oz) boneless turkey breast joint, skin removed
2 teaspoons dried mixed herbs
1 onion, quartered and stuck with cloves
2 tablespoons plain flour
300 ml (½ pint) chicken stock
4 tablespoons Madeira or Marsala wine or sweet sherry
salt and freshly ground black pepper

❶ Preheat the oven to Gas Mark 4/180°C/fan oven 160°C or according to the cooking instructions given with the meat.

❷ Rub the turkey with the herbs and some salt and pepper.

❸ Place the onion in a roasting tin and position the joint on top of it. Cover with foil and roast for 1¼–1½ hours. Test if it is ready by inserting a skewer into the thickest part of the meat – the juices should run clear. If not, put the joint back in the oven for a little longer then test again.

❹ Transfer the joint to a carving tray, reserving the pan juices, cover with foil and leave to stand while you make the gravy.

❺ Sift the flour into the pan juices and add the stock and wine or sherry. Boil briskly on the hob for 5 minutes. Season to taste.

❻ Carve the turkey and serve the sauce separately, or pour it over the sliced meat.

(1) Herb and lemon stuffing

Takes 20 minutes to prepare, 30–40 minutes to cook

| serves **6** | **POINTS** values per recipe **5** | calories per serving **60** | ❄ | **V** |

1 small onion, chopped very finely
100 g (3½ oz) fresh white breadcrumbs
finely grated zest of 1 lemon
3 tablespoons chopped fresh herbs (e.g. parsley, thyme, sage, rosemary)
1 egg, beaten
salt and freshly ground black pepper

❶ Preheat the oven to Gas Mark 4/180°C/fan oven 160°C.

❷ Place the onion in a small pan with a little lightly salted boiling water. Cover and boil for 5 minutes then drain.

❸ Combine the onion, breadcrumbs, lemon zest and herbs in a mixing bowl then season well. Add the egg and mix thoroughly. Divide the mixture into six and roll into small balls. Place on a baking tray or in a small, shallow cake tin.

❹ Cook in the oven for 30–40 minutes until firm and brown.

Turkey and cranberry burgers

Takes 25 minutes

| serves **4** | **POINTS** values per recipe **22** | calories per serving **288** | ❄ |

Turkey and cranberries are the perfect combination, so why just reserve it for Christmas?

450 g (1 lb) turkey mince
2 tablespoons cranberry sauce
50 g (1¾ oz) fresh wholemeal breadcrumbs
1 egg
4 spring onions, sliced thinly
salt and freshly ground black pepper

TO SERVE
4 burger buns
¼ Iceberg lettuce, shredded
4 tomato slices

❶ Place the mince in a large mixing bowl and add the cranberry sauce, breadcrumbs, egg, spring onions and seasoning.

❷ Using clean hands, combine the mixture together thoroughly.

❸ Divide the mixture into four and shape into burgers with your hands. Grill the burgers under a medium heat for 15 minutes, turning half way through the cooking time.

❹ To serve, split the burger buns in half and place a cooked burger in each with a little shredded lettuce and a tomato slice.

TOP TIP Burgers are always a welcome speedy snack, but home made ones are so much more tasty than the shop bought variety and have fewer **POINTS** values too. Why not make a double batch and freeze them individually, then you'll always have some fast food available!

Festive vegetable bourguignon

Takes 30 minutes to prepare, 35 minutes to cook

| serves **4** | *POINTS* values per recipe **16** | calories per serving **310** | **V** |

225 g (8 oz) sweet potato, peeled and cut into 5 cm (2 inch) chunks

225 g (8 oz) small parsnips, peeled and cut in half lengthways

225 g (8 oz) button mushrooms, left whole

225 g (8 oz) baby carrots, trimmed

8 shallots, peeled

175 g pack of baby leeks, trimmed

125 g (4½ oz) ready to eat prunes

125 g (4½ oz) vacuum packed cooked, peeled chestnuts

25 g (1 oz) plain flour

3 teaspoons olive oil

2 garlic cloves, crushed

400 ml (14 fl oz) hot vegetable stock

200 ml (7 fl oz) red wine

1 bouquet garni

salt

❶ Preheat the oven to Gas Mark 3/160°C/fan oven 140°C.

❷ Place all the vegetables, prunes and chestnuts in a large bowl. Sprinkle them with the flour and add salt to taste. Toss them until they are evenly coated.

❸ On the hob, heat a teaspoon of the oil in a large ovenproof saucepan or casserole dish. Add the garlic and a third of the vegetable mixture and heat until browned. Remove from the saucepan or dish and set aside, then repeat twice more until all the remaining oil and vegetable mixture has been used. Return all the vegetable mixture to the saucepan and pour the stock and wine over. Tuck in the bouquet garni and add salt to taste.

❹ Bring to the boil on the hob, cover, then transfer to the oven and bake for 35 minutes or until the vegetables are tender.

❺ Remove from the oven, divide the vegetables between four shallow bowls, discarding the bouquet garni, and set to one side but keep them warm. Return the saucepan or dish to the hob and rapidly boil the remaining juices, uncovered, until reduced to a syrupy consistency. Check to see if you need to add more salt then spoon the juices over the warm vegetables. Serve immediately.

Tropical celebration cake

Takes 45 minutes to prepare, 2½ hours to bake + standing + cooling

| makes **20** | *POINTS* values per recipe **79** | calories per serving **255** | ❄ | **V** |

Whether for Christmas, Easter or birthday celebrations, a cake is always appreciated.

low fat cooking spray
225 g (8 oz) sultanas
4 tablespoons brandy
100 g (3½ oz) ready to eat dried apricots, diced
100 g (3½ oz) glacé cherries, chopped roughly
100 g (3½ oz) glacé pineapple, diced roughly
50 g (1¾ oz) stem ginger, chopped finely
75 g (2¾ oz) dried apple rings, chopped roughly
50 g (1¾ oz) pecan nuts, chopped
finely grated zest and juice of 1 orange
finely grated zest of 1 lemon
100 g (3½ oz) polyunsaturated margarine
100 g (3½ oz) soft dark brown sugar
4 eggs
200 g (7 oz) plain white flour
a pinch of salt
3 teaspoons ground mixed spice

TO DECORATE
2 tablespoons reduced sugar apricot jam
225 g (8 oz) ready to roll white fondant icing
length of coloured ribbon

❶ Lightly spray a 20 cm (8 inch) round cake tin with low fat cooking spray. Line the base and sides with non stick baking parchment.

❷ Place the sultanas in a mixing bowl with the brandy, apricots, glacé cherries, glacé pineapple, ginger and apple rings. Stir well and leave to stand for 30 minutes.

❸ Mix in the nuts, orange zest and juice and lemon zest to the fruit mixture. Preheat the oven to Gas Mark 2/150°C/fan oven 130°C. Beat together the margarine and sugar until fluffy, and add the eggs one at a time, whisking well after each one. Sift in the flour and fold it into the mixture with the salt and mixed spice.

❹ Add the fruit and nut mixture to the flour and egg mixture and stir well. Spoon it all into the prepared tin and level the top with the back of a spoon. Bake in the oven for 2½ hours.

❺ Carefully remove the cake from the tin and allow it to cool completely on a wire rack – it's best to leave it overnight, covered with a clean tea towel.

❻ To decorate the cake, warm the apricot jam and brush it over the top and sides of the cake. Roll out the fondant icing on a clean surface and use it to cover the cake, pressing it down well with your hands. Place the cake on a cake board and tie a coloured ribbon around it. Re roll any fondant trimmings and cut out shapes to decorate the top depending on the occasion, for example, make stars or bells for Christmas.

TOP TIP To check if the cake is cooked or not, insert a metal skewer into the centre of the cake, count to five and then remove the skewer. If the skewer comes out clean, the cake is cooked. If any mixture sticks to the skewer, return it to the oven until it is cooked.

(3) Christmas mincemeat filo slices

Takes 20 minutes to prepare, 35 minutes to cook

| makes **16** | **POINTS** values per recipe **48.5** | calories per serving **185** | ❄ | **V*** |

*if using vegetarian mincemeat

There is no reason why we can't offer family and visiting friends festive fare over the holidays. Try these delicious, but easy, crisp flaky slices – a variation on mince pies which have all the usual delicious flavours but without the usual *POINTS* values! Serve with brandy butter, adding 1½ *POINTS* values per heaped teaspoon.

50 g (1¾ oz) walnuts, chopped
100 g (3½ oz) fresh brown breadcrumbs
50 g (1¾ oz) light muscovado sugar
400 g jar of traditional mincemeat
2 dessert apples, peeled, cored and chopped
175 g (6 oz) cranberries
grated rind of 1 orange
50 g (1¾ oz) half fat butter, melted
270 g pack filo pastry, thawed
icing sugar, for dusting

❶ Preheat the oven to Gas Mark 5/190°C/fan oven 170°C.

❷ Mix together the nuts, breadcrumbs and sugar. Line the grill pan with foil, and spread the mixture out over the pan. Cook under a preheated grill for 2–3 minutes, stirring from time to time until the crumbs are toasted. Leave to cool.

❸ Mix together the mincemeat, apples, cranberries and orange rind. Stir in the crumb mixture. Lightly brush a 23 x 33 cm (9 x 13 inch) Swiss roll tin with the melted butter. Layer three sheets of filo in the base, then spread with half the mincemeat mixture. Arrange three more pastry layers on top, spread the remaining mincemeat on top and finally cover with the remaining pastry. Brush the top with the remaining butter. Use a sharp knife to trim around the inside edge of the tin, discarding any overhanging pastry.

❹ Bake for 35 minutes or until the pastry is crisp and golden. Cool in the tin before dusting with icing sugar and cutting into 16 slices. This is best served at room temperature.

TOP TIP Read labels carefully on food. Now that there are so many varieties of mincemeat available at Christmas, it is not surprising that very often the fat and calorie content go up with the price! Buy a traditional recipe that offers fewest *POINTS* values and check whether it contains animal suet if you wish to cook a vegetarian version.

(5) Yuletide yogurt

Takes 10 minutes + 1 hour chilling

serves **2**	***POINTS*** values per recipe **10**	calories per serving **300**	**V**

*if using vegetarian Christmas pudding

Here is a novel way of getting that second helping of Christmas pudding. A little goes a long way with this fruity snack – ideal as a brunch too. Make an hour or so before you need it to give the sugar topping time to dissolve into a sweet glaze.

75 g (2¾ oz) leftover, cooked Christmas pudding, cold and crumbled
2 small satsumas
1 banana, sliced
75 g (2¾ oz) seedless grapes, halved
150 g (5 fl oz) low fat plain yogurt
1 tablespoon half fat crème fraîche
3 teaspoons dark muscovado sugar

❶ Put the crumbled pudding in a bowl. One at a time, hold the satsumas over the bowl to peel and segment them – allowing any juice to soak into the pudding. Chop the flesh and add it to the pudding together with the banana and grapes.

❷ Mix together the yogurt and crème fraîche. Carefully fold through the fruit mixture. Divide between two glass dishes. Sprinkle on the sugar, cover and chill for 1 hour.

(2) Spiced cranberry and orange warmer

Takes 10 minutes + 5 minutes standing

serves **6**	***POINTS*** values per recipe **12**	calories per serving **135**	**V**

This fruity drink, suitable for all the family, will surely bring inner warmth to a chilly winter's night.

1 litre (1¾ pints) cranberry juice
300 ml (½ pint) freshly squeezed orange juice
2 cloves
1 cinnamon stick (approximately 5 cm/2 inches)
2 teaspoons demerara sugar
1 orange, halved and cut into slices

❶ Place all the ingredients except the sliced orange in a saucepan. Heat gently for 5 minutes without letting the liquid boil. Switch off the heat and leave to stand for 5 minutes.

❷ Carefully strain into a large heatproof jug, add the orange slices and serve in heatproof glasses or tumblers.

TOP TIP If you have a slow cooker, transfer the heated juice, with the spices, to the preheated pot. It will keep warm for several hours without spoiling. Simply ladle out as required.

VARIATION This is a great non alcoholic drink, but for a special glow why not add 2 teaspoons brandy per glass? Allow 2½ ***POINTS*** values per serving.

Cranberry spiced slice

Takes 20 minutes to prepare, 40 minutes to cook

| makes 10 | *POINTS* values per recipe 34.5 | calories per serving 190 | ❄ | V |

Cranberries start to appear in the shops towards the end of November. Make the most of this shiny red berry – there's more to it than cranberry sauce! Delicious with a cup of freshly brewed coffee.

FOR THE TOPPING

25 g (1 oz) butter
75 g (2¾ oz) granulated sugar
250 g (9 oz) fresh cranberries
50 g (1¾ oz) pecan nuts or walnuts, chopped coarsely

FOR THE CAKE

75 g (2¾ oz) self raising flour
2 tablespoons cocoa powder
¼ teaspoon baking powder
½ teaspoon ground allspice
3 eggs
75 g (2¾ oz) caster sugar
1 tablespoon vegetable oil

❶ Preheat the oven to Gas Mark 4/180°C/fan oven 160°C. Line the base and sides of a 23 cm (9 inch) round loose bottomed cake tin with greaseproof paper. Smear the paper with the butter, and then sprinkle 1 tablespoon granulated sugar evenly over the base and sides of the tin. Mix the remainder with the cranberries and nuts and scatter over the base of the tin.

❷ To make the cake, sieve together the flour, cocoa powder, baking powder and spice in a bowl. Whisk the eggs and sugar together in a bowl set over a pan of simmering water. Keep whisking until a trail is left on the surface from the beaters.

❸ Fold in the flour in batches, taking care not to knock the air out of the egg mixture. Finally, trickle and fold in the oil.

❹ Pour the cake mixture into the tin. Place on a baking sheet and bake for 40 minutes or until the cake is springy to the touch and a skewer inserted in the centre comes out clean. Cool for 10 minutes before turning the cake out on to a cooling rack and removing the paper lining.

TOP TIP It is important to spend the time whisking the eggs and sugar until the mixture is really like mousse and foamy.

VARIATION For an Orange and Cranberry Spiced Slice, replace the cocoa powder with its weight in flour, and add the grated zest of 1 large orange with the eggs and sugar. Drizzle the juice of the orange over the skewered cake once cooked. The *POINTS* values remain the same. Serve warm.

$6\frac{1}{2}$ POINTS VALUE Christmas cake

Takes 45 minutes to prepare + soaking (optional), 4 hours to bake

| makes **16** | *POINTS* values per recipe **102** | calories per serving **380** | ❄ | **V** |

Friends and family alike will love this low point Christmas cake.

250 g (9 oz) sultanas
4 tablespoons rum or brandy (optional)
low fat cooking spray
175 g (6 oz) candied peel, chopped
175 g (6 oz) glacé cherries, halved
100 g (3½ oz) blanched almonds, chopped
250 g (9 oz) currants
225 g (8 oz) plain flour
100 g (3½ oz) polyunsaturated margarine
100 g (3½ oz) soft brown sugar
2 tablespoons clear honey or black treacle
grated zest of 1 lemon
grated zest of 1 orange
4 eggs
½ teaspoon salt
½ teaspoon mixed spice
½ teaspoon grated nutmeg
2–4 tablespoons skimmed milk

FOR THE ICING
4 tablespoons reduced sugar jam
227 g ready to roll royal icing

❶ Soak the sultanas in the rum or brandy, if using, for up to 2 hours before you make the cake.

❷ Preheat the oven to Gas Mark 2/150°C/fan oven 130°C. Spray a 20 cm (8 inch) round cake tin with the low fat cooking spray, line twice with baking paper that stands a good 2.5 cm (1 inch) above the top of the tin, and spray again. Tie a band of baking paper around the outside of the tin to give extra protection from over browning.

❸ In a large bowl, mix all the fruit and nuts with a tablespoon of the flour to coat them. Cream the margarine and sugar together until light and fluffy, then mix in the honey or treacle and the lemon and orange zest.

❹ Beat the eggs with a whisk until thick and foamy and add a little at a time to the margarine mixture beating well after each addition. If the mixture shows signs of curdling then mix in a tablespoon of flour and keep beating. Sift the rest of the flour, salt and spices together and lightly fold into the mixture.

❺ Fold in the fruit and nut mixture and just enough milk, if necessary, to make a batter moist enough to drop off a spoon if given a good shake.

❻ Spoon into the prepared tin and make a deep hollow in the centre to ensure that the cooked cake has a flat top for icing. Cover with a double layer of baking paper and bake for 4 hours or until a warm skewer inserted into the middle comes out clean.

❼ Allow the cake to cool in the tin for 1 hour before placing on a cooling rack.

❽ To ice, place the cake on a board. Warm the jam in a pan with 4 tablespoons of water until melted. Brush the sides and the top of the cake with the jam.

❾ Roll out the royal icing to a piece large enough to cover the whole cake like a blanket. Drape over the rolling pin to place over the cake and then press gently on to the cake's surface and trim the edges. From any left-over icing or trimmings, cut out decorations in the shapes of a star, holly leaf or Christmas tree. Paint with food colourings and place on top. Alternatively, decorate with sprigs of holly.